JAPAN'S WORLD WAR II BALLOON BOMB ATTACKS ON NORTH AMERICA

ROBERT C. MIKESH

号

SMITHSONIAN INSTITUTION PRESS

City of Washington

Originally published in the Smithsonian Annals of Flight series

Printed in the United States

97   96   95   10   9   8   7   6

Library of Congress Cataloging in Publication Data
Mikesh, Robert C.
Japan's World War II balloon bomb attacks on North America
(Smithsonian annals of flight, no. 9)
Bibliography: p.
1. World War, 1939-1945—Aerial operations, Japan. 2. Balloons. I. Title. II. Series.
TL515.S5 no. 9   [D792.J3]   613.13'08s   [940.54'49'52]   72-8325

Contents

Foreword

Mr. Mikesh has compiled the most complete account ever published on one of the most bizarre and obscure chapters in modern warfare. Never before had the United States received attacks launched directly from an enemy shore. Never before had the American public been more in the dark about the nature of an attack, due to tight security measures.

Although the damage caused by these balloons was slight, their psychological impact was real, and history should not overlook their use. Mr. Mikesh became an authority on this subject through personal interest while serving in the United States Air Force. He studied this subject in detail while stationed for a number of years in Japan and supplemented these findings with our own military records. Now a retired major, Mr. Mikesh has written authoritatively on the subject in a variety of publications, and this *Annals of Flight* represents the culmination of years of fastidious research on a fascinating subject.

Michael Collins, Former Director
National Air and Space Museum

Acknowledgments

My first note of thanks must go to a close family friend, Justis Webb, who sparked my interest in this subject in 1945. He had been an Air Force pilot flying C-47s on forest-fire patrols relating to the defense against the ballon bombs and gave me the first hint that such a weapon existed. Little was said about the balloons even after the war, but my curiosity continued to grow.

In 1960, while researching another subject at the Aerospace Studies Institute, Maxwell AFB, Alabama, I casually mentioned by interest in Japanese balloon bombs to Miss Marguerite K. Kennedy, Chief, Archives Branch. Through her kind assistance, she and her staff searched their files and discovered a vast amount of material on this subject. It was at this time that I decided to prepare a definitive study about the Japanese balloon bombs, since little information other than brief accounts had ever been published. After ten years of collecting, researching, and interviewing many that were associated with the balloon bomb, I feel satisfied that as much relevant material as possible has been located for incorporation into this document. This could not have been possible had it not been for the help of a great many people.

During my final four-year period in Japan, I was able to meet and discuss with many of those having firsthand knowledge of the balloon program. Among these were former Major Teiji Takada, engineer for the balloon project, who provided invaluable material and insight from his personal observations. For this, I am grateful. My thanks to former Colonel Susumu Nishuira, now Chief, Japan War History, Defense Agency, Ichigaya, Tokyo, for locating and making available to me the many Japanese documents on this military operation. I frequently think of the many laborious hours spent by my good friends, Mr. Tosuke (Jack) Magara, and Mr. Shorzoe Abe in providing the translations needed to make these documents meaningful to me. Mr. Mannoske Toda, publisher of *Koku Fan,* made his material on balloon bombs available for this study. Mr. Eiichiro Sekigawa was most generous as a close personal advisor and in providing many opportunities for acquiring this material in Japan through his affiliations in the aviation-writing and publishing field. Mr. Yoshiji (Eddie) Osawa was a great inspiration as a friend, having had firsthand experience as a boy in the hand manufacture of the balloons, and in relating his wartime experiences.

Mr. James A. Winker, vice president of Raven Industries, Inc., provided a large amount of material. Through his company's association in the manufacture of balloons, material had been acquired about Japan's balloons and this file was made available to me. This provided many heretofore missing details for which I am very grateful. Colonel C.V. Glines, USAF (Ret.) gave continuing encouragement in seeing this project to reality due to his interest in the subject, and was most helpful in some of its preparation. Dr. Clarence S. Ross, formerly with the United States Geological Survey had been the mineralogist that evaluated the sand carried as ballast by the balloons. During our interview, he disclosed a great deal of information never before recorded on this subject which adds greatly to this study. When Mr. Frank Lara, public relations manager of the Weyerhaeuser Company, in Klamath Falls, Oregon, learned of this documentation project, he offered eager assistance with photographs and accounts surrounding the six casualties of the balloon bomb that occurred in the company's lumbering area.

Meteorologists James F. Andrews and Philip F. Clapp of the National Weather Service, Suitland, Maryland, were very helpful in their technical assistance relating to information about the upper air currents that carried the balloons across the Pacific.

The help and encouragement of my colleagues at the National Air and Space Museum cannot go without special mention. Namely, these are Messrs. Louis S. Casey, Robert B. Meyer Jr., C. Glen Sweeting; and Louise Heskett of the Smithsonian Institution Press, who edited this manuscript. Mr. Roger Pineau, a former NASM colleague, has given unstintingly of his knowledge of Japanese history, language, and lore. His counsel and translations have been invaluable.

The cover art work, which adds a touch of Japanese flavor to this study, was expertly done by Mrs. Keiko Hiratsuka Moore and is most appreciated.

To all these people, and to any who may have been inadvertently overlooked I give my sincere thanks.

Robert C. Mikesh
15 June 1972

Introduction

The strategy of large-scale modern warfare, which leans very heavily upon the Intercontinental Ballistic Missile, may well have been touched off by the epic attack of the Doolittle Raiders against Tokyo in April 1942. Ironically, this mission also sparked the invention of the world's first intercontinental weapon. The concept of balloon bombs might have changed the course of the war in favor of the Japanese had it been pursued with more vigor and tenacity.

The "Doolittle Raid" during World War II was planned against Japan to "cause confusion and impede production." The Americans knew that the bomb loads of these sixteen B-25 Mitchell bombers could not do enough physical damage to invoke any permanent delay of the war. But there were high hopes that the appearance of American planes over the Japanese home islands would be such a psychological blow that the enemy might change their strategy of conquest to the benefit of the Allies.

Doolittle had no way of knowing then, but the bold raid he led hastened the end of the war by encouraging the Japanese to engage the Americans at Midway and lose disastrously. In a desperate attempt to find a means of reprisal, the Japanese conceived a method to strike directly at the American continent. Their plan was simple; launch balloons with incendiary and anti-personnel bombs attached, let them travel across the Pacific with the prevailing winds, and drop on American cities, forests, and farmlands.

It took over two years to design the balloons, bombs, and automatic dropping mechanism. Japanese scientists, spurred on by the fury of the militarists and the need for a return gesture which would regain them the "face" they believed they had lost in the eyes of the world, worked day and night to solve the technical problems. Finally, on 3 November, 1944, the first of more than nine thousand bomb-bearing balloons was released. It is estimated that nearly one thousand of the death-dealing balloons must have reached the North American continent. They were found over an area from Attu in the Aleutians, as far east as Michigan, and reaching southward to Mexico. They took the lives of six Americans and caused other damage, but their potential for destruction and fires was awesome. Even more important, if the extent of this remote kind of bombing had been known generally, the shock to American morale might have been worse than any potential material damage.

Historians have tended to make light of this use of man's oldest air vehicle, seemingly a pathetic last-ditch effort to retaliate against the United States. It was, however, a significant development in military concept, and it preceded today's intercontinental ballistic missiles launched from land or submarines. Had this balloon weapon been further exploited by using germ or gas bombs, the results could have been disastrous to the American people.

Figure 1. The large Japanese paper bombing balloon in the rear of the exhibit hall in the Smithsonian Institution's Arts and Industries Building in 1972. This one was recovered at Echo, Oregon, on 13 March 1945 after making the Pacific crossing. (72-2993)

Origin and Development

The Unexpected

From widespread reports during 1944-1945, along with paper and metal fragments, United States military authorities began piecing together a fantastic story. The following are four isolated but typical incidents that led the military to become concerned.

A father and son on an early morning fishing trip were just settling down when they observed a parachute or balloon-like object drift silently by and over the nearby hill. Moments later an explosion echoed through the valley leaving only a small trace of smoke coming from the direction in which the object had disappeared. By the time the two reached the area of the incident, fragments of paper were the only thing unusual in the silence of the north woods.

The attention of two farmers at work in their field was diverted to a sudden explosion in a nearby field and an eruption of a cloud of yellow smoke. They moved cautiously to the scene, only to find a small hole in the ground with metal fragments nearby. There was no evidence as to how this mysterious object was delivered.

A mother tucking her sleeping child in for the night was shocked by a sudden flash of light through the window followed instantly by the sharp crack of an explosion in the silent darkness.

Ranchers coming over the top of a hill near where they had camped the night before, discovered a partially inflated balloon entangled in the scrub brush. It had no bombs, but somewhere along its journey it had discharged its lethal cargo.

A Japanese offensive had been launched using balloon-borne incendiaries and anti-personnel bombs carried by wind currents to the American continent. World War II air raids by enemy planes usually allowed ample warning for people to take cover, but this new threat against a nation that had never experienced an air offensive was being launched in silence without any form of warning by an air vehicle dating back to 1783.

Figure 2. United States military and government officials inspect a Japanese balloon near Burns, Oregon, where it was discovered on 23 February 1945 (USAF 30776AC).

The threat of an unheralded explosion with attendant death and destruction could panic the nation. There was no way of knowing the possible extent or duration of balloon launchings. In the dry season, widespread scattering of incendiary bombs could literally burn out the vast forests of the Pacific Coast. This was Japan's intended purpose along with the associated psychological effect upon the American people. Then, there was the possibility of using balloons to spread germ warfare—a far greater menace.[1] The threat to the nation was more frightening than the military or other government agencies dared reveal to the public, and so the situation was played down as much as possible.

For the Japanese, this was not a simple air operation. It took two years of testing and preparation before the first bomb-carrying balloon was launched from Japan. But they drew upon a technology that dated back much further.

Early Balloon Programs

At the siege of Venice when no position could be found for siege guns, it was decided to use balloons for bombardments. This was during the Italian War of Independence, 1848-1849, when Austrian Lieutenant Uchatius undertook the technical development of such a means of attack. Hot air balloons of thin paper were used. These balloons could carry bombs weighing thirty-three pounds for a half hour, and were dropped by means of a time fuse. The point of departure of the balloons was determined by the direction of the wind. No great material damage was done to the enemy, though one of the charges burst in St. Mark's Square. An unexpected shift of the wind drove some of the balloons back to the besiegers and their use was abandoned.

The Japanese idea of a balloon bomb originated in 1933, when Lieutenant General Reikichi Tada, of the Japanese Military Scientific Laboratory, was assigned to the head the "Proposed Airborne Carrier Research and Development Program" which was to investigate and develop new war weapons. Several revolutionary weapons were already under consideration. The "I-Go-Weapon" was a small wire-controlled, manless tank which could attack enemy pillboxes and wire entanglements. The "Ro-Go-Weapon" was a project to develop a rocket propellant. Still another was a "death-ray" weapon which could kill enemy soldiers at close range with a charge of electricity.

---
[1] Though possible, the Japanese did not consider this aspect.

Figure 3. Japanese paper bombing balloon (A 37180C).

Of all the items under consideration in this series, the "Fu-Go-Weapon" seemed to offer the most promise. The idea was based on small, four-meter-diameter (13.1 feet), constant-altitude balloons capable of carrying explosives. The wind was to carry the balloons approximately seventy miles to enemy positions, where the bomb load would be released by a time fuse. It was hoped that the results would approximate in range and accuracy those of the heavy guns used by the Germans against Paris in World War I. This project appears to have been stopped in 1935 and never completed.

Figure 4. A faulty ballast-dropping mechanism caused this balloon to land, without dropping its bombs, near Tremonton, Utah, on 23 February 1945. Little damage was caused to the envelope.

An excursion into the Japanese language is warranted here to ensure an understanding of weapon nomenclature. The term "Go" in this sense, is the equivalent of "Number." In the case of the "I-Go-Weapon," "I" (pronounced "EE") is the first character of the Japanese I, Ro, Ha syllabary. "Ro-Go-Weapon" could be properly translated to "Weapon No. B" or the second in this series. "Fu-Go" is the thirty-second character of the syllabary. These weapons are exotic by nature to be sure, but considering the time of their development, it is

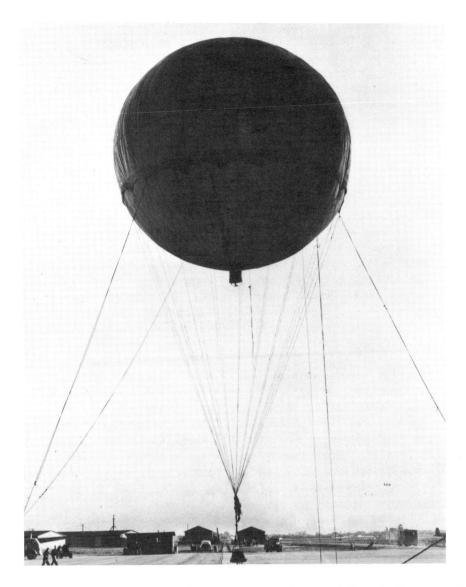

Figure 5. Americans were quick to inflate a recovered Japanese balloon for inspection of all components. This balloon was retrieved intact near Alturas, California, on 10 January 1945. (U.S. Army photograph, SC-226135)

unlikely that they were preceded by thirty-one advanced-weapon ideas. "Fu" happens also to be the first character in "Fusen," meaning "Balloon," and this probably explains why this weapon was termed "Fu-Go."

Although conceived in the mid-1930s, ten years before its actual use, the idea of the balloon weapon system was never totally shelved. Limited research continued with the idea of using it to scatter propaganda leaflets in enemy territory, taking advantage of lower altitude winds. Balloons large enough to silently carry foot soldiers into enemy lines at night was also con-

sidered. Thus, the element of surprise as obtained with the present-day paratrooper would be realized.

With the onset of World War II, reorganization of army units placed the balloon-weapon research under the 9th Military Technical Research Institute,[2] and the former Army Scientific Laboratory was discontinued. The degree of priority given to the "Balloon Bomb"

---

[2] Commonly called Noborito Research Institute, located where the Odawara Express Line crosses the Tama River on the southwest side of Tokyo. Flight testing eventually moved to Ichinomiya on the Chiba Peninsula, to later become one of the operational launch sites for the balloon offensive.

project cannot actually be determined. Its importance was enhanced, however, by the Doolittle Raid on 18 April 1942, along with other methods or reprisal against the American continent. As the threat of air attacks against Japan became a continuing reality, with the American continent yet untouched, revengeful attack methods gained in importance.

Other considerations included one-way bombing attacks by long-range, land-based bombers. There were, however, no suitable airfields within practical range of the United States. Japan kept trying until the end of the war to develop a bomber capable of non-stop flight from Japan to the United States, one way if necessary. An interim measure of launching small, bomb-carrying airplanes from submarines was studied and one attack was made by one Yokosuka E14Y1 aircraft (Allied Code name "Glen"), the night of 9 September 1942, starting small forest fires near Mt. Emily, Oregon. Improved planes and submarines were developed, but there was no promise forthcoming of any appreciable number of such attacks, and primary efforts were diverted to other projects.

The research project of balloon weapons was continued in an effort to bomb the American continent. In March 1943, a six-meter (19.6 feet) balloon with a desired range of 3,000 kilometers (1,863 miles) was developed which flew 1,000 kilometers (621 miles) between the west and east coasts of Japan. It was found that this model could stay in the air for more than thirty hours at an altitude of 8 kilometers (26,247 feet). This type of balloon was further developed so that all components could be loaded on board submarines through their restrictive hatches. The balloon was to be inflated on the deck of the submarine, then attached to it was an automatic altitude-control device, a time mechanism for releasing a bomb, and one 5-kilogram incendiary bomb. The balloon was to be launched from the submarine on the surface at night approximately 620 miles from the United States giving it a flight time of about ten hours. Success probability for flight was quite good provided a flight was confined to daylight or night time, but not to both. Gas expansion and contraction caused by day-night temperature change would create problems with longer flight times.

So much importance was attached to this effort, that it was made a joint army-navy research project. The navy would equip two submarines[3] at the Kure Naval Base with balloon launching facilities, while the army would concentrate on balloon development and ordnance to be dropped from them. Two hundred balloons were assembled for this operation.

Plans were nearing completion when the submarines being modified for this mission were recalled for the Guadalcanal operation, resulting in the discontinuance of this project in August 1943. The acute war situation dictated that every available submarine was needed to transport weapons and food to the starving Japanese troops in the islands.

As the noose of Allied might drew tighter around the Japanese, the necessity for some way to carry the fight to the enemy's shores became more urgent. The development of longer range balloons launched from Japanese soil seemed to be a logical answer.

---

[3] Submarines I-34 and I-35 were so equipped.

Transpacific Balloon

Meteorology

The idea of "inter-continental free-flight balloons" was feasible. There was a continuity of wind patterns over Japan and over the American continent. The 9th Military Technical Research Institute sought the advice of the Central Meteorological Observatory in Tokyo, where meteorologist H. Arakawa was asked about the feasibility of using these wind currents. He was also asked the following questions. At what altitude should the selection be for the balloon bombs to travel? What seasons are most favorable to the project? How many days would it take for balloons released from Japan to reach the central zone of the United States? What would be the diffusion of the constant-level balloons over North America?

Fairly accurate data was available to Mr. Arakawa concerning winds from the Asian continent that crossed over Japan, but winds over the Pacific were relatively uncharted. The phenomenon of local wind speeds of 200 to 300 kilometers per hour (120 to 185 miles per hour) at certain latitudes and at higher altitudes of around 12 kilometers (39,370 feet) in the winter months were being studied and needed further research. Little was known of air currents above 13.5 kilometers (44,291 feet).

Between 1942 and 1944, facts were collected and studied from the seven Japanese radiosonde stations at Sendai, Niigata, Wajima, Yonago, Fukuoka, Shio-no-Misaka, and Oshima (see Figure 6). From these records of the upper air in scattered regions of Japan, supplemented by surface weather observations from ships and islands over the Pacific Ocean, Arakawa was able to develope logical wind-flow patterns extending across the Pacific. These "rivers of fast moving air"—later called "jet streams"—which had been studied in Japan did not become a major matter of American interest until high-level, B-29 bombing raids against Japan were well under way in 1944. Beginning in October, the jet stream is quite strong over or south of Japan above the 9.1-kilometer (30,000-foot) level, and it attains maximum velocity from November through March. Use of this jet stream increased the chances of success in the employment of this balloon weapon.

The method used to estimate the upper wind pattern near 12 kilometers, very briefly, was to assume that the decrease of temperature with altitude over the Pacific was given. Then, using surface weather observations, it was possible to calculate the pressure field at this altitude. The horizontal gradient of pressure, together with the latitude, then gives the geostrophic wind speed.

From these calculations, the flying course of the balloon, its speed, and its diffusion were analogized, and optimum launch locations were determined. It was noted that the upper air stream varied considerably in curve as it reached the American continent. The air stream in the American continent area would generally flow to the southward, while this could vary as the balloon would descend as it neared its destination. The time required for a balloon to transit the Pacific Ocean was estimated to be from thirty to one hundred hours with an average time of sixty hours.

To substantiate these findings and determine the feasability of spanning the Pacific, some two hundred paper balloons[4] were launched during the winter of 1943-1944. These meteorological tests were a joint effort along with engineers whose task was to develop the transpacific balloon. Attached to each experimental balloon was radiosonde equipment to collect and transmit upper air information to stations in Japan. None of the balloons reached the United States nor was that the intention. From the information derived and further calculations, answers to the meteorological questions were obtained and Japanese engineers—encouraged by the probability of success—proceeded with enthusiasm.

Engineering Obstacles

The main concern that faced engineers for the "Fu-Go Weapon" was to develop a method of keeping the balloon flying at a fairly high altitude for the fifty to seventy hours it would take to cover the 6,200 miles of ocean. If the balloons were launched in the daytime,

---

[4]These were the balloons that had been placed in storage for some future use after the submarine-launched, balloon operation was terminated.

Figure 6. Radiosonde plotting-station locations in Japan used for upper wind study in 1945.

continuous sun radiation in clear skies at the upper altitudes would cause the gas temperature to rise from an average of 0°C. to more than 30°C. in the afternoon on the side of the balloon facing the sun. This would expand the balloons to the bursting point. At night, the reverse would be true since the temperature is usually −50°C., and at 33,000 feet atmospheric pressure is approximately one-fourth the pressure at sea level. The balloon would thus lose excessive altitude as it lost buoyancy.

By using the experience gained from the six-meter-diameter balloons, the problem was solved by the installation of a gas discharge valve at the base of the balloon, and attaching an ingenious automatic system for dropping ballast. The size of the balloon had to be large enough to support the increased load of ballast and the metering valve, which together controlled the balloon altitude. To obtain this added endurance for increased range, a ten-meter-diameter (32.8 foot) balloon was determined as optimum for this requirement. The buoyancy of the ten-meter balloon was about five times that of the six-meter balloon. The balloons, usually made of three and four layers of tissue paper cemented together to form a gas-proof sphere, were inflated with hydrogen to a capacity near 19,000 cubic feet. When filled, they had a lifting capacity of 1,000 pounds at sea level and about 300 pounds at 30,000 feet. The balloon envelope was encircled by a scalloped cloth band to which numerous shroud lines were attached, and these were tied together below in two large knots. From these knots, the bombs and ingenious ballast release mechanism were suspended.

The altitude-control mechanism was developed under the supervision of Technical Major Otsuki of the Noborito Research Institute. This device consisted of a cast-aluminum wheel from which bags of sand were hung. By means of aneroids and a small battery, a release fuse attached to two sandbags was ignited whenever the balloon reached a preset minimum altitude. The balloon then would rise again to approximately 38,000 feet, and be carried along by the higher winds. It would sink to the minimum desired altitude—around 30,000 feet—as the gas slowly escaped or was cooled. Two more sandbags were then dropped, as the process was repeated. When all thirty-two sandbags were expended, the balloon would discharge its load of bombs and destroy itself by a small demolition charge. The number of cycles required was calculated, based upon forecasted wind speeds, and appropriate settings were made to position the balloon over the American continent for bomb release.

The next engineering problem was unusual temperatures and pressures that the balloon equipment would encounter. All Japanese army equipment was designed to operate to extremes of −30°C.; however, at −50°C. at the 260-millibar pressure level, rubber components and springs lost their elasticity. Also electrical batteries were greatly reduced in power output, and ballast-dropping explosives lost reliability because of the low pressure. Therefore, considerable research was directed toward high-altitude explosives, antifreeze batteries, and the use of solar heat and other insulation methods.

As these tests were being made between May and August 1944, nearly all dry ice in Tokyo—for testing cold resistance of components—was diverted to this project. It was a common practice for scientists working on this program to personally check daily on the status of the ever-dwindling supply of dry ice.

Tests conducted to determine direction and altitude of the balloon, skin and gas temperatures, gas pressure, ballast dropping, altitudes gained by the balloon, and the functioning of the gas-relief valve with relation to air-pressure expansion were all monitored by radio. For this reporting purpose, many types of radiosonde equipment had to be developed.

Probably the greatest difficulty for the Japanese was developing a radiosonde that could operate consistently under varying stratospheric conditions. The responsibility for development of such a system went to the Japanese 5th Army Technical Research Institute. The primary purpose of the radio equipment would be to report the balloon's flying course, its altitude, and to measure the balloon's inside pressure. In addition, it would also provide data on the balloon's descending and ascending flight. This would give an added indication of

when the ballast was being dropped. The first tests were conducted from Chiba Prefecture, east of Tokyo.

At the time, there was no radiosonde known which could operate for the desired length of time in stratospheric conditions. Success of the balloon-development program depended upon this radio-reporting equipment. The development of a power source of adequate durability and the selection of proper frequencies caused the most trouble. In order to check the functioning of radio equipment during these experimental flights, various models of the radiosonde apparatus were developed and suspended from balloons.

Many agencies became involved in the development of radiosonde equipment. Included was the Army Weather Bureau that assigned their most experienced member, Engineer Yuasa Matsumoto, who developed no less than ten experimental radiosonde transmitters for this effort.

After considerable research, an adequate radio set was finally developed. Attached to a balloon and released in free flight, it operated for eighty continuous hours, relaying back the valuable flight information. The radio fell silent when the balloon reached a point at longitude 130° west; however, engineers were exuberant with the results. They concluded that a balloon could cross the Pacific in three days during the winter period from November to March.

The radiosonde equipment developed for observing the balloon's flight course produced a continuous wave, moderated by a multivibrator. This piece of equipment had a power output of two watts with an alternating A and B frequency which worked on an alternating cycle. "A" frequency would operate ten minutes and rest ten minutes. While "A" was resting, "B" would operate and vice versa.

Navy Balloon

Paralleling the army's paper-balloon program but with a later start, the Imperial Japanese Navy also began a study of balloon bombs to utilize a skin of rubberized silk. This became known as the "Internal Pressure Type" balloon. Both balloon designs were of similar size, but the payload of the silk balloon was not as great due to the greater weight of the envelope.

Instead of controlling altitude by the release of ballast and venting excess gas pressure, as was the case with the paper balloon, the navy's version was sealed after filling, being designed to keep its volume constant, yet strong enough to tolerate pressure changes with temperature and altitude. Flight altitude was relatively stable, making this one of the more favorable features of this balloon concept. Consistent flight altitude made for

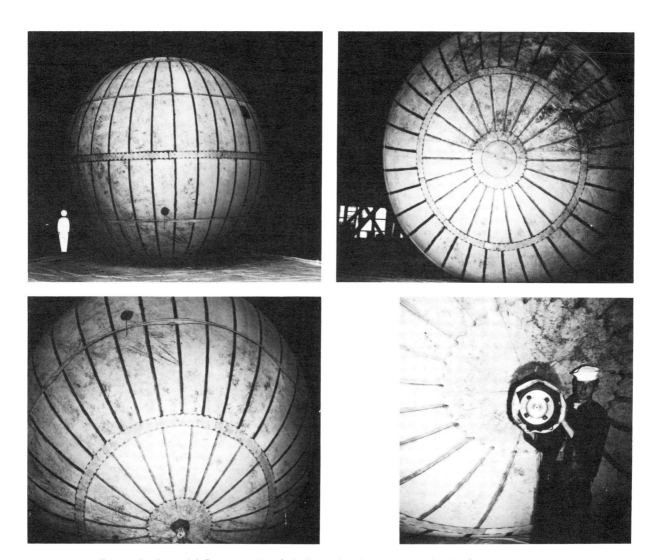

Figure 7. Imperial Japanese Navy's balloon development consisted of a rubberized-silk envelope. Due to the weight, its payload was much less than the paper balloon developed by the army. (U.S. Air Force photograph, 30770).

better plotting of weather data and tracking the balloon flight path; however, readings of gas pressure became their highest by 3:00 P.M. daily during flight and many balloons failed at this point in time. A safety valve was then installed on subsequent balloons that would vent hydrogen at 50 millimeters Hg (by mercury barometer)[5] which resolved the problem. This retained sufficient pressure, causing little effect upon buoyancy. A light-weight and simple ballast-dropping mechanism was also employed.

The internal pressure-type balloon for the navy was originated by Rear Admiral Naneko Kichisaboro, head of the Sagami Naval Arsenal. Captain Ogawa, head of the

arsenal's research and development, and Professor Tatsusuke Nakamura, of the Imperial University at Nagoya, collaborated in the design study.

In the spring of 1944, all army and navy balloon research was again consolidated. The navy's balloon project, supervised by Technical Lieutenant Commander Kiyoshi Tanaka, was moved to, and became part of, the Army's 9th Military Technical Research Institute. The continued development of this balloon was assigned by Major General Sueyoshi Kusaba, the head of the project, to Technical Major Takada with Commander Tanaka of the navy to assist him. At this time, the army assigned "B-Type" as the designation for navy-developed balloons, while continuing with the term "A-Type" for the paper balloons.

---

[5] United States technical evaluation shows this figure to be 35 millimeters of mercury.

Despite continued research in this balloon concept, the results were disappointing. The buoyancy of the B-Type balloon was nearly zero at the ground, causing ascent to be quite slow. While the A-Type balloon reached the 10,000 meter altitude within forty minutes, it took the B-Type from two, to two and one-half hours to reach the fast-moving jet stream at that altitude. This also made launching rather difficult when there was any wind, for the balloon and its payload would be damaged as it skipped over the ground before rising.

Usually, from two to three B-Type balloons were released daily from Ichinomiya carrying radiosonde gear for experimentation and tracking. Finally, it was concluded that mass production of this balloon was impractical because of the heavy drain of manufacturing resources and materials otherwise used for explosives. One engineer on the project stated: "There was no other reason than this lack of material for this more durable and reliable balloon skin, that the noncritical paper-material balloon was placed in service." Consequently, production was limited to three hundred of the B-Type balloons before this navy-originated concept was abandoned.

Traditionally, neither Japanese military service wished to be subservient to the other or, for that matter, willingly share in the other's project. Therefore, the Japanese navy continued with balloon research under a new concept which consisted of balloons capable of carrying a crew to effect some flight control. The bombs were attached individually to small balloons and used as ballast weight for release to drift independently to the targets, and thus achieve stabilization in altitude of the main balloon. A model test was conducted at the Fujikura Industries Company in Tokyo, but never went beyond the testing stage before the war ended. Other exotic ideas were brought up, but never materialized.

Accelerated Development

With test flights showing positive results, the research group concluded that "the attack against the North American continent with balloons flown from the Japanese homeland was not impractical." The group added to this conclusion, however, that many problems still remained to be solved before the balloon operation could be successfully implemented.

Lieutenant General Shinoda, director of the Noborito Research Institute, related the status of development to his superior, General Mimura, Commander of Weapon Administration Bureau, and suggested that for the timely solution of unsolved problems, cooperation of eight institutes would be necessary. These should be under the control of General Mimura, to be assisted by the Itabashi Research Institute of the Army Arsenal, as well as scientists outside the army. This suggestion was approved, and a program for accelerated research for components of balloon bombs was prepared.

The first meeting of scientists and technicians concerned was held at the Weapon Administration Bureau at Wakamatsu-cho, Ushigome-ku, Tokyo. The date of this event is not recorded, but it is presumed to have been held in May 1944. Major General Sueyoshi Kusaba, who had been the key figure in the development of the Fu-Go Weapon from the early beginning led the study group. He briefly related the current development status of the program, and then took four hours to deliberate on the problems yet to be solved. Each research institute was asked to assist in the areas of their expertise.

Shortly following this conference, each research institute received approval for study under the authority of the commander of the Weapon Administration Bureau for the Fu-Go Weapon. A two-million-yen budget was allotted to the Noborito Research Institute for the project. The research group headed by General Kusaba took charge of flight experiment, coordinated and conducted the "Fu-Go Research Project" from each of the other institutes, and thus became the focal point of the entire project.

Consultants on general affairs were Dr. Hidetsugu Yagi, Dr. Sakuhei Fugiwhara of the Central Meteorological Observatory, and Dr. Tatsujiro Sasaki of the Aeronautical Research Institute. Dr. Masaichi Majima of the Tokyo Imperial University acted as chairman for the project.

Manufacture

While experimentation continued in the early part of 1944, manufacturing facilities for balloon envelopes were being set up in seven different locations in the vicinity of Tokyo. By manufacturing the balloons in this general area, distance to the launch sights was reduced. This minimized creasing the envelope and other damage in shipping that could increase the possibility of gas leakage. Components for the release mechanism were made by several manufactures and shipped to the launch sites along the nearby coastline for final assembly.

The factory operations were supervised by a Captain Nakamura and a civilian technician. Some of the industrial firms concerned and connected with the operation were the Mitsubishi Saishi (paper factory), the Nippon Kakokin Company, and the Kokuka Rubber Company. The panels were then sent to subcontractors

Figure 8. Japanese technicians struggle with an experimental balloon operation at the Sagami Arsenal in the spring of 1944.

Figure 9. Surface wind was the greatest detriment while filling the balloons and releasing them for flight.

who assembled the envelopes into the finished products.

The program called for 10,000 balloons to be mass produced in time for the approaching fall and winter winds of 1944-1945. Mr. Teiji Takada, a former technical major at the Noborito Research Institute, clearly defines the magnitude of such an undertaking.

> To cope with the requirement of 10,000 balloons, all materials were considered with reference to their critical resources compared to the research necessary for substitute materials. Ten thousand balloons would carry about 1,800 tons of articles, while the total weight of hydrogen cylinders to be prepared to fill these balloons equally amount to 1,200 tons. Visualizing that hundreds of slowly burning fuse cords, along with hundreds of thousands of electric detonators were required, we could fully perceive what the number 10,000 means.

One of the earlier technical problems that had to be solved was to design an inexpensive gas-proof balloon bag of noncritical material that could be mass produced. After much experimentation, it was found that good results could be obtained from tissue paper made from fibers of the *kozo* bush, a member of the mulberry-tree family, but very similar to the American sumac.[6] The paper was to be obtained from the hand-manufactured-paper companies all over Japan; however, with these various sources, the standard of quality could not be controlled. The strength of the paper was dependent chiefly upon the fiber which had to be uniform, yet it was necessary to have it be very light. The size of the sheets also varied with each manufacturer.

Lieutenant Ito of the Noborito Institute made a technical breakthrough when he developed a mechanical method of processing the *kozo* fiber into paper. Not only could sheets of desired size be manufactured, but a mechanical method of laminating the layers was also developed. This was a revolutionary event in the age-old hand process of Japanese paper manufacturing.

For gas-proofing the paper, many types of sealers were tested; one produced a wax paper and another, natural gum. Both were too heavy. An adhesive called *konnyaku-nori,* made from a type of Japanese potato,[7] proved to be best for joining the seams. At a time when there was an acute food shortage in Japan, it was not unusual for laborers to be caught stealing the powdered *konnyaku*[8] that was used to make the paste sealant, as this was a very stable food substance. Coloring was added to the paste to let those engaged in the application know how evenly it was applied to ensure gas-proofing.

After the paper—now laminated—was dry, it was inspected for possible flaws. This was done in a dimly lit room that was floored with frosted glass having electric lights placed beneath it. Sheets of raw paper placed individually upon the lighted floor became translucent with a bluish color caused by the adhesive. Areas of light color showed up as being insufficiently pasted, while even a hair on an inner layer from a pasting brush was quickly spotted. Defects were circled with chalk; and in an adjacent room, patches were applied over these areas.

The raw, handmade, standard-weight paper made from the mulberry tree was fifteen grams per square meter. Strength was gained by laminating the three and four layers of paper alternately lengthwise and breadthwise. Next, the panels were softened by dipping them in a solution of soda ash, a water wash, and then a solution of glycerine. The glycerine wash was soon replaced with calcium chloride and other softeners since munitions powder had a higher priority for the glycerine than the balloon project. After the panels were dried, the edges were trimmed and panels were pasted together on a spindle form, the upper part first, then the lower part. Each balloon consisted of 600 separate pieces of paper, all having to be glued together with no allowance for gas leakage. After the relief-valve neck was installed in the lower hemisphere, both hemispheres were joined together by an encircling scalloped band which was glued on. This band formed the suspension skirt to which the shrouds were attached.

A large floor area was required for the shaping and final assembly room. All protrusions—not only on the floor but around the walls—were carefully wrapped with paper, to protect the balloon skin from damage. It was difficult to detect skin abrasions once the balloon was assembled. Girls that were making the balloons were instructed not to wear hairpins, to have closely trimmed fingernails, to wear socks even in the midsummer heat, and to use gloves despite the fact that their work required manual dexterity.

To test the balloons for possible leaks, buildings large enough to house the inflated thirty-three-foot-diameter envelopes were required. Large theaters and *sumo* wrestling halls were ideal, but more were needed and had to be built for the testing which added considerably to the cost of the balloons. Such buildings as the Nichigeki

---

[6] In addition to *kozo* (Broussonetia Kazinoki), the *matsumata* (Edgewortia Papyrifera) tree was also used in the manufacture of Japanese paper for the balloons.

[7] Also commonly called *arum root.*

[8] In later years, as war tensions eased, Japanese lightheartedly referred to the "Fu Go" as the "Konnyaku bakudan" ("Konnyaku bomb").

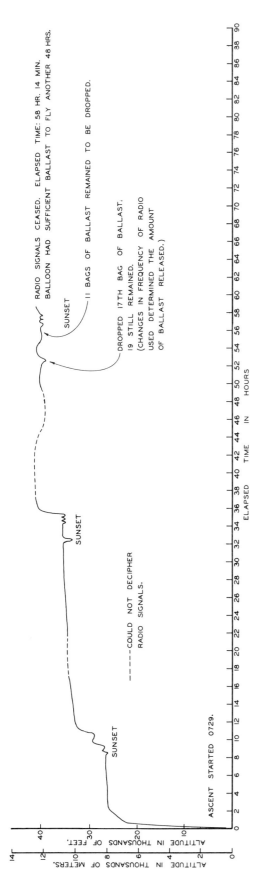

Figure 10. Japanese recording of paper-balloon test flight of 29 August 1944.

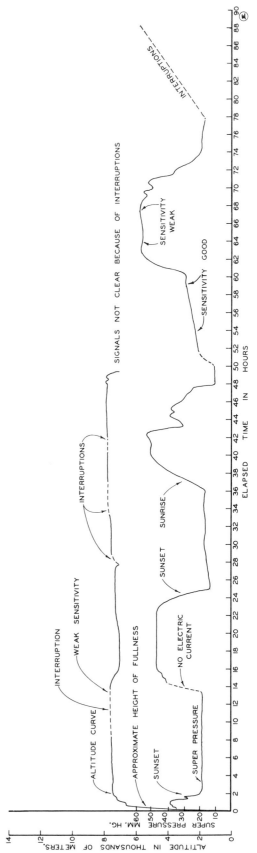

Figure 11. Rubberized-silk balloon flight recording conducted by Japanese technicians on 29 September 1944.

14

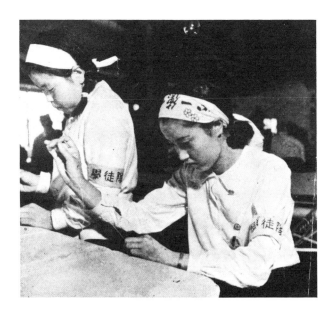

Figure 12. Great numbers of Japanese high-school girls were used in the delicate work of pasting and stitching the balloon envelope.

Music Hall and the Toho Theater in Tokyo, and Kokugi-Kan Wrestling Hall in the Tokyo borough of Asakusa were used.

For the test, the balloon was filled with air blown into it at a pressure of 120 meters of water column, after which it was sealed. After twenty-four hours, it was checked for leakage. Those that were satisfactory were then coated with a protective lacquer.

The earlier paper balloons were made in factories, but when the demand reached its peak, the factories processed the paper and made the majority of the panels. The panels were then sent to subcontractors who assembled the finished product.

Figure 13. Large arenas and theaters were used for balloon production and inflation testing. One building was the Nichigeki Music Hall, a familiar modern-day landmark in downtown Tokyo.

Figure 14. A skyward view of an inflated balloon held captive by its shroud lines. The gas relief valve is shown at the base of the envelope. (A 37180F)

Figure 15. The Japanese paper balloons were 32 feet in diameter and, when fully inflated, held about 19,000 cubic feet of hydrogen. (A 37180F)

In numbers, school children were the greatest labor force on this project. During wartime, school hours were short in order that the remainder of their day could be devoted to the war effort. Thousands of Japanese had a part in making these balloons, but officially they were never told of their purpose. Even when word about their intended use would filter down, no one believed it.

Two years of experimentation and some 9,000,000 yen (more than 2,000,000 prewar dollars) were spent on the manufacture of balloons. Still another source quotes the original price per balloon at 10,000 yen, roughly $2,300 at the prewar rate of exchange, but this cost was considerably reduced as production increased. It is difficult at this time to accurately determine from these figures what actual costs were involved.

Balloon Launch Sites

While the fabrication of the balloons was underway, the army formed a new operational unit called the Special Balloon Regiment, under the command of Colonel Inoue. Its responsibility was to prepare launch sites, establish direction-finding station locations, prepare for gas-production facilities, and train personnel in the launching of the balloons.

Three general site locations were selected along the lower half of Honshu's eastern seaboard. These areas were chosen because of nearby rail lines and favorable terrain. Also, the coastal sites lessened the possibility of damaging Japanese property through flight mal-

functions. Of the thousands of balloons released, only two returned to Japan. Both occurred on 13 March 1945, twenty fours after launching, but they fell in snow and caused no damage. The first landing was reported near Hakodate on Southern Hokkaido, while the second was located in Akita Prefecture. The northern regions of Japan were ruled out as launch sites because of the possibility that balloons might stray into Kamchatka, a Soviet Union territory, and cause an international incident.

Balloon launch locations and their unit and functions that occupied them were as follows:

Otsu, Ibaraki Prefecture

Command Headquarters.
First Battalion (composed of three squadrons). Total strength: 1,500.
Weather Unit (in connection with the Army Weather Bureau).

Ichinomiya, Chiba Prefecture

Second Battalion (composed of three squadrons). Total strength: 700.
Test Release Unit.

Nakoso, Fukushima Prefecture

Third Battalion (composed of two squadrons). Total strength: 600.

Hydrogen-generation plants became the key to launch operations. The Nakoso and Ichinomiya sites depended upon the gas being transported in tanks from distant Kanto Plain companies, such as Showa Denko (a chemical and electric company still operating under this

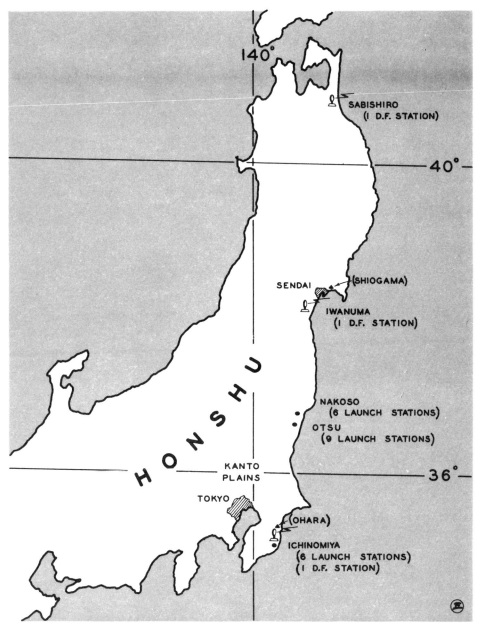

Figure 16. Balloon launching sites and flight-following stations.

name). The Otsu site, however, was capable of generating its own hydrogen from the beginning of the operation.

Launching Operations

To achieve the greatest effect from the balloons based upon weather forecasts, the following proposed launch schedule was worked into the plan, based on the possibility that 15,000 balloons would be available (actual balloon operations are shown for comparison).

Date	To be launched	Approximate number launched
November 1944	500*	700
December	3,500	1,200
January 1945	4,500	2,000
February	4,500	2,500
March	2,500	2,500
April (early)	0	400
Total	15,000	9,300

*Anticipated difficulties with the new program accounted for this low figure.

17

Figure 17. Balloon launching complex at Otsu after the war. Note the shelter caves in the side of the hills and the sea in the background. (U.S. Army photograph, SC 284816)

Figure 18. The United States Army's First Cavalry Division, on maneuvers in occupied Japan on 22 April 1947, discovered these former balloon launching sites at Otsu. (U.S. Army photograph, SC 283906-S)

Figure 19. The seclusion of the hills aided as a windbreak when filling the balloons, as well as security from detection. (U.S. Army photograph, SC 283809-S)

Figure 20. These rail lines once brought the envelopes, munitions, and other supplies needed to operate the balloon offensive at Otsu. (U.S. Army photograph, SC 283910-S)

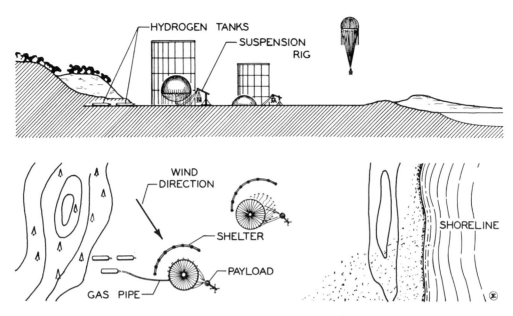

Figure 21. Profile and plan-view of balloon launching facility at Ichinomiya.

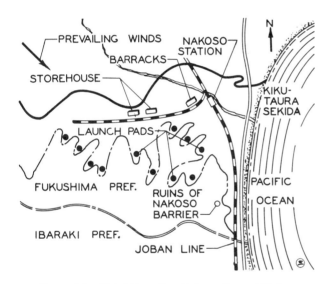

Figure 22. Third Battalion Release Base at Nakoso.

The plan further called for the following balloon ordnance:

15-kilogram bombs	7,500
5-kilogram incendiaries	30,000
12-kilogram incendiaries	7,500

Depending on the choice, from two to six pieces of ordnance could be carried on each balloon. (Far less than the proposed number of balloons were released; however, the ordnance sent aloft was in the above proportions.) According to one Japanese source, the balloon load varied from a minimum of about twenty-

Figure 23. Rusty tanks for the hydrogen generating plant is all that remains of this former balloon launch site. Only Otsu had its own gas facilities. (U.S. Army photograph, SC 284185)

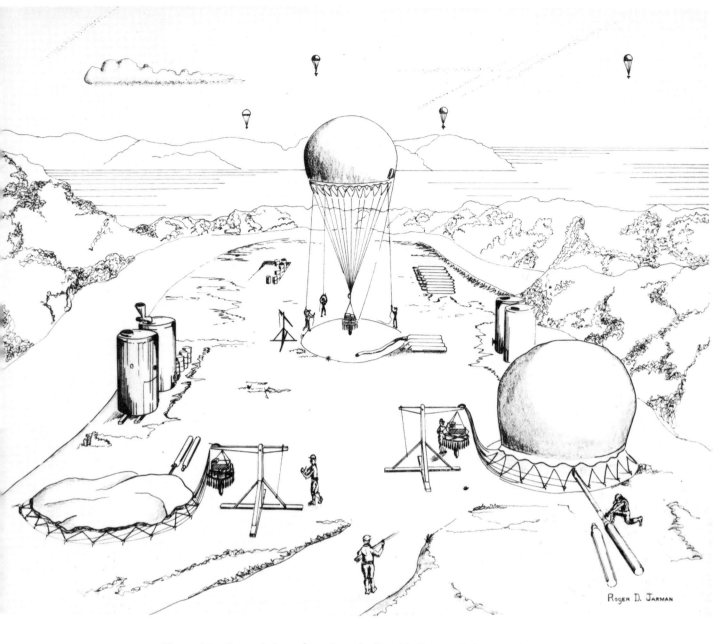

Figure 24. General view of one launch site with three pads in operation.

five pounds to a maximum of about seventy pounds, with the average about fifty pounds. Such variations in loading were apparent in recovered balloons. Typical maximum loading was one fifteen-kilogram high-explosive bomb or one twelve-kilogram incendiary along with four five-kilogram incendiary bombs.

It was on the birthday of a former ruler, Emperor Meiji—3 November 1944—at 0500 that the air assault of balloon bombs was officially begun against the continental United States. This attack could not have started at a more favorable time for the Japanese. The new season brought strong winds in the jet stream to propel the balloons. The American public was just becoming uneasy about the German V-2 rocket attacks against

England, with thoughts that extended ranges might have them falling on American cities. Kamikaze attacks in the Pacific created added fear in showing the extent to which the enemy might go with new weapon threats. Above all, the balloon bomb, as a new weapon system, could provide a much-needed morale boost for the Japanese people.

Mr. Teiji Takada, a former staff member of the Noborito Research Institute and one of the scientists on the Fu-Go Project recalled his thoughts of the mass launching of these balloons after his months and years of toil in developing this weapon system. "When the planning stages of the Fu-Go was over and a large-scale release was started, the bombardment by the United

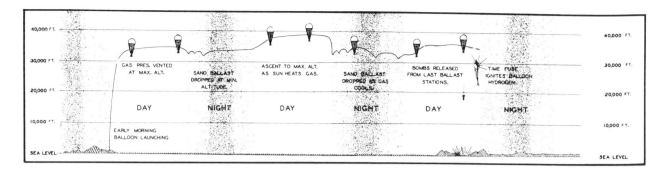

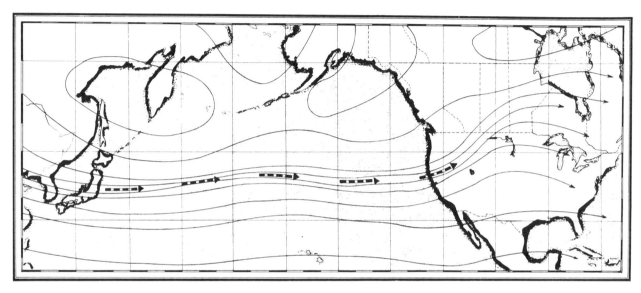

Figure 25. A typical balloon flight profile is shown above; below, a typical jet stream in winter months.

States air forces was growing in its violence. Every night, the sky was red in reflecting the flame of conflagration and the people who lost their homes by fire crowded around us, increasing in number day by day. This scientist continued: "Trembling with fear of the raging fire, we desired to make use of the fire hoping its violence to be fully displayed in the enemy country. We exerted our full effort to realize our inconsistent desire. What contradicting objectives we were driven to by the war!"

Major General Sueyoshi Kusaba, charged with the Fu-Go Weapon operation, estimated that he had five months of favorable winds to prove the effectiveness of this new weapon. With the initial allocation of ten thousand balloons, he knew that it would not be an easy matter to launch this number successfully in the time allotted. Considering that it took from thirty minutes to an hour to prepare one balloon for flight at any launch pad, many pads had to be in operation at each major launch site. To accomplish these launchings during the most favorable months of the year when the winds were

of greatest velocity, the days had to be clear and with relatively no surface wind. In ascending through rain, snow, and even some clouds, the balloon accumulated moisture which froze—adding much weight—and prevented it from reaching operating altitude. It was vitally important that the balloon ascend into the fast-moving jet stream so that the programmed release of the ballast and dropping of the bombs would occur over the North American continent. Failure to reach the jet stream meant that the balloon would self-destruct before spanning the Pacific.

The best time to launch was just after the passing of a high-pressure front. Launching conditions were unsuitable if a high-pressure front was approaching, or a low-pressure front had just passed.

Filling the balloon with hydrogen was most difficult and dangerous on windy days. Desirable wind conditions for launching could be expected only three to five days a week. Even then, it could be done for only several hours at a time, usually just before the onshore breezes at sunrise. On occasion, some launches took place in the

Figure 26. Partially inflated balloon, with its bomb load, in flight over the Pacific Ocean drifting toward the American continent. (U.S. Army photograph, SC 226132)

responsible for these harsh measures. Ironically, the bombs used with the balloons came from normal army ordnance channels and retained the standard Japanese markings. All components were destined for destruction if all worked properly, so the reason for the absence of Japanese markings on certain portions of the completed weapon is questionable.

Where people are concerned, however, there will always be infringements on security. Despite elaborate measures otherwise taken, it was learned that as the launching operation neared completion a strange custom had developed whereby Japanese soldiers had been placing their personal *samhara* into some secluded fold of the balloon just as it was about to be launched. These were amulets usually given to the soldier as he left for war to be carried on his person as a Shinto prayer for protection against accident. As all eyes would watch the ascending balloon after so much effort had been applied to the operation, this mindful prayer must have been with all the observers.

Very tight security measures were enforced during launching operations. Farmers and fishermen were barred from the surrounding area, but as this was an air operation, it was impossible to prevent some people from seeing the balloons ascend; however, the sparsely populated areas along the coastline eased the security problem. Little was said of the operations and no mention of the flights were ever published. People with a hint that the balloons were destined for the United States found the thought too fantastic to believe. The absurd nature of this highly secret operation added immeasurably toward safeguarding it.

Eye witnesses recall that these launches were an unforgettable sight. When freed from the ground a balloon was only partially filled, to allow for expansion to full inflation at 16,000 feet. At release, the unfilled concave lower portion of the envelope, with its many ropes dangling from the perimeter, greatly resembled a giant jellyfish. The white, and sometimes light blue, color in the early morning sun enhanced this illusion. Their silent drifting off into space, broken only by an occasional rattle of the slack paper, was eerie. The balloon was visible for only several minutes following its release before it faded away as a spot in the blue sky like a daytime star.

Flight Following

Launching the balloon was one thing, but the flight path of each group of bombs had to be followed to determine that it had a good chance of reaching North America. While the launch sites were being prepared, the

early evening. In the period from November through March, about fifty suitable days were all that could be anticipated and two hundred balloons were the maximum that could be launched from the three site complexes per day. The launching of one balloon normally required a crew of thirty men.

Setbacks in the program were greater than expected. Despite this, March which had been programmed for the smallest number of launchings because of uncertain wind currents and generally poor surface weather, actually produced nearly three thousand balloon operations, the largest of any month.

Security was an important factor during the launching operations as well as in the manufacturing of the balloons. While Japanese markings and stamps would normally be used to facilitate assembly of components, alphabetical letters or figures were used instead. No trace of origin of the balloon was to be allowed and inspectors were reprimanded on any infringement of this rule. Fear of disclosing the manufacturing location or launch site which would result in reprisal attacks by B-29s were

Army Special Balloon Regiment also established Radio Direction Finding installations with the aid of the 5th Army Technical Research Institute. This Institute was given the task of providing the electronic assistance for the project. These sites were located at Sabishiro[9] in northern Honshu; Iwanuma, along the central east coastline; and Ichinomiya, at the launch site southeast of Tokyo.

While balloon operations were in progress, an occasional balloon carrying radiosonde equipment instead of bombs was launched. This light-weight radio equipment produced a continual signal on a preselected frequency. As the bearing of each transmitting balloon was plotted from predetermined frequencies, the Direction Finding stations were able to monitor the flight paths quite accurately.

Beginning with the first launching on 3 November 1944, the easterly tracks were followed for nearly two thousand kilometers (1,240 miles) and indicated a fairly constant speed during the eight to ten hours of tracking. Beyond that distance, direction and distance had to be assumed. For more accurate tracking, a station was established on Sakhalin Island, north of Hokkaido, and tracks could then be followed for more than thirty hours. With these plottings, the Japanese were fairly certain that the balloons were capable of reaching the United States.

Like the bombing balloons, a release mechanism dropped the load of radio equipment when out of range of the home station and before the balloons reached their destination.

---

[9]Not far from Misawa Air Base and Hachinohe in northern Honshu, is Sabishiro, noted for its seashore which was chosen by the American flyers, Clyde Pangborn and Hugh Herndon, for the starting point of their transpacific flight in October 1931. Their Bellanca monoplane, "Miss Veedol," made the first nonstop flight from Japan to America in 41 hours and 12 minutes.

American Reaction

The first discovery of a Japanese balloon introduced more mystery than immediate concern. This sighting was on 4 November 1944, when a navy patrol craft spotted what looked like a large fragment of tattered cloth floating on the sea, sixty-six miles southwest of San Pedro, California. The unidentified debris was hauled on board, and was soon determined to be a rubberized-silk balloon with a heavy undercarriage attached. Ironically, this balloon was from the first group launched on 3 November (Japan date), just two days earlier—*two* days because of the international dateline.

The apparatus, still connected to the undercarriage of the balloon, consisted of a small radio transmitter. The equipment bore Japanese markings and indicated that something new and mysterious had been introduced into these final months of the war.

The incident was reported through military channels, but it caused little concern until two weeks later when a second fragment was salvaged from the ocean. Within the next four weeks, balloons were found in Wyoming and Montana. This clear evidence of a new and unexpected balloon-borne weapon gave rise to increased concern, and the assistance of all government agencies—national, state, and local—was immediately summoned. Forest rangers—state and national—were ordered to report any balloon landings and any recoveries of portions of balloons or their undercarriages.

Of more and immediate vital concern was the reaction of the American people to this unorthodox weapon. What psychological response would develop from realization that the American continent was under sustained enemy air attack for the first time in the history of the United States? What panic might result from the thought that countless silently moving balloons could be drifting across our continent, randomly discharging their bombs into homes and factories? The threat was a potential reality.

And what of this load? The destructive explosive power was measurable, but what of the incendiary threat? With our great forests along the entire West Coast and extending inland, a massive incendiary raid during the dry season could envelop the entire area in one gigantic, uncontrolled holocaust. From this alone, the loss of lives, property, and building materials would be beyond imagination.

There were further possibilities to consider. Biological agents could also be transported by balloon, spreading disease among the people and livestock over large areas of the United States.

Panic—based on the fear of the unknown potential of this new weapon—was in itself a vital concern to responsible agencies in the United States government. The best defense against panic was to say as little as possible about this new menace, and play down any local anxieties.

Publicity

The lack of publicity associated with the balloon bombs had still another far-reaching effect. After the announcement in the newspapers of discovery of a Japanese bombing balloon in Thermopolis, Wyoming, elaborate and apparently successful efforts were made to prevent the Japanese from gaining any knowledge of bomb damage and balloon sightings in the United States. It was obvious that the Japanese would be eager to know the effects of the attacks, and that information on the courses followed by the balloons and the areas hit by the bombs would enable them to evaluate and improve their techniques.

The one incident that had made the papers in the United States was indeed known in Japan. The Chinese newspaper *Takungpao* had picked up the report from American sources and repeated it in late December 1944. For the moment, this proved to the Japanese high command that the concept was sound and allowed the program to continue. To their chagrin, however, no further comments on the balloons were found, although United States, Russian, and Chinese reports were continually screened.

Considering the widespread dispersion of the balloons—reported from the Arctic Circle to the Mexican border—the primary goal was to prevent the Japanese from learning of their effectiveness.

On 4 January 1945, the Office of Censorship requested newspaper editors and radio broadcasters to

Figure 27. Wind catches a recovered balloon like a parachute. Note the arrangement of the gores on the lower surface with the relief valve in place. Photo taken on 23 February 1945. (29907 AC)

Figure 28. Elaborate measures were sometimes taken in the recovery of these balloons for closer inspection. Here, Indians chop down a treed balloon which landed harmlessly on 29 March 1945 at Pyramid Lake, Nevada. (29906 AC)

give no publicity whatsoever to balloon incidents. This voluntary censorship was adhered to from coast to coast, a remarkable self-restraint in a free-press-conscious country. Three months later, in a strictly confidential note to editors and broadcasters, the Office of Censorship stated:

> Cooperation from the press and radio under this request has been excellent despite the fact that Japanese free balloons are reaching the United States, Canada, and Mexico in increasing numbers . . . . There is no question that your refusal to publish or broadcast information about these balloons has baffled the Japanese, annoyed and hindered them, and has been an important contribution to security.

The success of the security measures was indicated by an Associated Press release on 2 October 1945, following the surrender, that contained these comments:

> The Japanese listened eagerly to radio reports, hoping to hear of the bombs' effectiveness. But American editors voluntarily kept the information to themselves and so discouraged the Japanese that they abandoned the project.
> The Japanese learned of only one bomb landing in the United States. It was one which came down in Wyoming and failed to explode.

The voluntary censorship, ironically, made it difficult to warn the people of the bomb danger. The risk seemed justified as weeks went by and no casualties were reported. On 5 May 1945, however, five children and a woman were killed near Lakeview, Oregon, by a balloon bomb which exploded as they dragged it from the woods.

This tragic accident caused the government to abandon its campaign of silence. On 22 May, a joint statement by the war and navy departments was issued which described the nature of the balloon bombs and warned all persons not to tamper with any such objects that they might find. The balloon weapon was said to constitute no serious military threat to the United States, because the attacks were "so scattered and aimless." The statement continued by stating "that the possible saving of even one American life through precautionary measures would more than offset any military gain occurring to the enemy from the mere knowledge that some of his balloons actually have arrived on this side of the Pacific." An educational campaign was instituted at once to warn all persons, particularly children, of the danger of tampering with strange objects found in the woods.

United States Military Countermeasures

Initial Detection

The Fourth Air Force, with headquarters at Hamilton Field, just north of San Francisco, had been charged with the air defense of the West Coast of the United States as late as 1943. The threat of air attack had long before faded and the Fourth Air Force became primarily involved in training combat replacements. After recovery of the first few balloons in November and December 1944, the responsibility for a study, along with a defense against the bombing balloons, was assigned to this command. This unexpected new menace placed them once again in the air-defense business.

Instead of the earlier possible threat of massive assaults by aircraft from Japanese carriers, now the enemy vehicle was a paper balloon. The seriousness of this new threat, however, cannot be overemphasized. This unique Japanese offensive weapon of an unknown magnitude had tremendous possibilities, and to what extent these might be developed, the situation was critical. By mid-December 1944, a military intelligence project was well underway to evaluate this new weapon system, but even then there were only a few isolated incidents from which to draw information.

Aside from the first discovery on 4 November 1944 of a rubberized-silk balloon off the coast of California, the first report of a balloon incident to reach the Fourth Air Force was that of a paper balloon discovered on 11 December near Kalispell, Montana. On 19 December the Western Defense Command reported that a bomb crater had been discovered near Thermopolis, Wyoming. As an explosion in that area had been heard during the night of 6 December, it was thought that the crater had been caused by a balloon-borne bomb on that date. On 31 December, twelve days after the bomb-crater discovery in Wyoming, a paper balloon and some apparatus were discovered near Estacada, Oregon.

Local military authorities were puzzled by these discoveries. When the Kalispell balloon was reported, for example, it was thought to have been launched from a Japanese relocation center or from a German prisoner-

of-war camp in the United States. Since the first balloon discovered off San Pedro in early November carried what was believed to have been radio and meteorological equipment, local officials concluded that it was perhaps a weather balloon which had been blown across the ocean. With the discovery of the Wyoming bomb crater in December, however, attention was directed toward the theory that the balloons carried bombs, for the fragments found near the crater were determined to be parts of a high-explosive bomb of Japanese manufacture. During the first two weeks in January 1945, four more balloons were recovered, and from them additional information was obtained which led to the conclusion that the balloons actually were a new, Japanese offensive weapon.

The War Department was kept fully informed of each reported balloon incident and, on 4 January 1945, the

Figure 29. Aerial photograph of a Japanese balloon in flight over Reno, Nevada, taken by a pursuing Bell P-63 King Cobra from Walla Walla Army Air Field, Washington, on 22 March 1945.

Chief of Staff designated the commanding general, Western Defense Command, as coordinator for all balloon intelligence activities in the Seventh, Eighth, and Ninth Service Commands. Concurrently, the commander, Western Sea Frontier, was designated coordinator for balloon intelligence activities over ocean areas.

Reports clearly indicated that one purpose of the balloons was the dropping of either incendiary or antipersonnel bombs. Other possibilities were not overlooked, however, and toward the end of March 1945 the War Department prepared a statement listing the various uses to which the balloons might be put. The following six possibilities were enumerated in order of importance.

1. Bacteriological or chemical warfare, or both.
2. Transportation of incendiary and antipersonnel bombs.
3. Experiments for unknown purposes.
4. Psychological efforts to inspire terror and diversion of forces.
5. Transportation of agents.
6. Anti-aircraft devices.

Firefly Project

It was concluded, however, that the greatest danger was not from the 32-pound antipersonnel bombs they carried, but the incendiaries which would be a serious threat to the West Coast forest regions during the dry months. One incendiary could ignite hundreds of square miles of valuable timber. As a result, Ninth Service Command, Fourth Air Force, and Western Defense Command joined in a plan for special assistance in fighting forest and grass fires. Under the provisions of this plan—named "Firefly Project"—a number of Stinson L-5 and Douglas C-47 airplanes, and approximately 2,700 troops—200 of them paratroopers—were stationed at critical points in probable hazardous fire areas for use in fire-fighting missions.

Lightning Project

When the possibility that the enemy might launch germ-carrying balloons was advanced, another plan, known as the "Lightning Project" was initiated, and army officials immediately advised the Department of Agriculture. Without fanfare, word was spread to health and agricultural officers, veterinarians, 4-H clubs, and agricultural colleges to be on the lookout for the first sign of any strange disease in livestock or crops. Stocks of decontamination chemicals and sprays were quietly shipped to strategic points in the western states.

Balloon Interception

The mystery surrounding the purpose of the balloons, however, did not delay the preparations of air defense plans. Uncertainty as to the enemy's intentions and the possibility of the balloons becoming a real menace, stimulated the development of countermeasures.

The first attempt by Fourth Air Force planes to search for a Japanese balloon occurred on 19 December 1944. Four fighter planes were directed by the Los Angeles Control Group on that date to search the Santa Monica area for a reported balloon. The planes were unable to locate their target. Although nearly five hundred aircraft were at various times dispatched in search of reported balloons between 1 December 1944 and 1 September 1945, only two balloons were ever shot down over the North American continent by planes. The first of these was brought down by a Lockhead P-38 from Santa Rosa Army Air Field on 23 February 1945, near Calistoga, California. The second balloon was trailed on 22 March by fighter planes all the way from Redwood, Oregon, into Nevada. Passing over Reno, the balloon finally settled in nearby mountains. Determined to make a capture, one fighter pilot landed his plane to continue the pursuit by automobile, but the balloon released some ballast and bombs in the hills and ascended again over the plain. One of three Bell P-63s from Walla Walla Army Air Field circled overhead and destroyed the balloon by gunfire.

The bullets generally used on these missions were a new type of experimental ammunition known as the "headlight tracer." These were designed to inflict little or no damage to the balloon when it fell to the ground.

The navy was also involved with balloon interception in support of this operation. Corsair pilots, for instance, recall the many hours spent in the cockpit on runway alert for possible scramble pursuit of the balloons.

The first Allied territory in the balloon flight path was the Aleutian Islands, where army and navy air forces were based. Throughout early April, daily flights of the bomb-carrying balloons passed over this region, and anti-aircraft fire and combat air patrols succeeded in shooting down some of them. On 13 April alone, navy F6F Hellcat fighters shot down nine balloons at altitudes of between 30,000 and 37,000 feet over Massacre Bay on the eastern tip of Attu Island; however, that was less than half the number that escaped their interception and proceeded on their eastward journey. This indicated an increase in the tempo of the operation; whereas in reality it marked the final flights of the balloon program.

The poor interception record was a result of inaccurate sighting reports, bad weather, and the very high altitude at which the balloons traveled.

Figure 30. A Lockheed P-38 Lightning is credited for bagging the first Japanese balloon over American territory. This occurred on 23 February 1945 near Calistoga, California. (A-103110)

Figure 31. After tracking a Japanese balloon from Redwood, Oregon, to central Nevada, one of the three Bell P-63 King Cobras was credited with the second kill on 22 March 1945. (71-1252)

Figure 32.   Grumman F6F Hellcats had a field day in early April 1945 over the Aleutians when nine balloons were shot down. (A-47332)

Figure 33.   Pilots spent many hours on cockpit alert waiting to be scrambled for balloon interceptions. Vought F4U Corsairs were used in large numbers, as were other types. (A-103981)

Most of the activities connected with readiness for immediate air defense of the West Coast had been almost completely deactivated. Nearly all of the early-warning radar stations had been placed on a caretaker basis, the Ground Observer Corps had been deactivated, and the Information and Filter centers had been closed. With no aircraft warning service in operation, the Fourth Air Force was unable to guard the West Coast against any surprise air attack. No combat planes were kept on ground alert, and a defense force could be organized only after several hours' warning. Anti-aircraft defense was likewise very limited. With regard to possible means of defense against balloons, the following statement came from a military planning meeting held at the Western Defense Command Headquarters on 17 January 1945:

> Balloons are relatively slow moving in comparison with aircraft; therefore, provided they are observed there will probably be time to take counteraction before they are over vital areas. Should balloons approach in hours of darkness, visual observation will not be effective. It is not yet known whether radar will detect them. Defense against this weapon must be based on a means for their early detection and their prompt destruction over water or waste land by aircraft and antiaircraft artillery. This may involve reactivation, partial or complete, of radar screens, ground observer corps, and information and filter centers or similar installations, as well as provision for alert fighter units and additional 'alert' antiaircraft artillery.

Consideration was, therefore, given to a plan for positioning a fighter-training group in each of the vital defense areas as a defense force. Groups in an advance stage of training could be selected for this purpose, and could be rotated after two weeks or one month. In addition, the Ground Observer Corps could be partially reactivated, and radar stations might be operated for early-warning purposes.

It is interesting to note that despite interception of some balloons above 30,000 feet, a majority of the sightings were at no more than 20,000 feet, and this was presumed to be their normal operating altitude. The exact opposite was true, since those discovered at 20,000 feet and below were actually malfunctioning balloons. Additionally, Americans did not fully appreciate the effectiveness of the jet stream above 30,000 feet for calculating the intended altitude and time of flight for the balloons. Consequently, all balloon calculations by the Americans were based upon the lower level winds with vast variations in flight path and time of crossing.

As an interesting aside, a project was initiated in December 1944 in the United States for a free balloon to fly from China over the Pacific Ocean to obtain meteorological data. A study of the various problems involved was in progress at the close of the war before the flight was accomplished, and the project was canceled in September 1945.

Captive-Balloon Experiments

As with every new weapon, a defensive system had to be developed. Radar detection of the balloons for aircraft interception appeared to be the standard solution for the slow balloons. In the opinion of several radar experts, the metallic valve of the balloon would be radar-visible, but the envelope itself would not be reflective. Chance of detection at 10,000 feet would be slight and at higher altitudes it would be impossible.

Several agencies became involved in experiments to determine the degree of radar reflectivity of the Japanese balloon system. Responsibility for a test program was divided between the Naval Airship Training and Experiment Command at the Chesapeake Bay Annex and the army's Camp Evans Signal Laboratory

Figure 34. This inflated balloon shows the geometry of the many paper gores which make up the gas-proof envelope. Nineteen shroud lines attached to the cloth skirt carry the gondola. (U.S. Navy photograph, 80-G-326353, in the National Archives)

south of Asbury Park, New Jersey. Tests began on 14 February 1945 at the Chesapeake Bay Annex when a metallic reflector equal to that of a balloon relief valve was sent aloft while attached to a ZMK barrage balloon moored to a small powerboat. Measurements of reflection were taken at distances of 4,000 yards and 8,000 yards utilizing a pulsed-signal generator and equipment developed originally for measurement of ship-target radar.

A noticeable echo generated by the motor launch that towed the balloon into position rendered the tests inaccurate. A rowboat was then used in order to reduce the echo problems, but it too met with little success.

Army engineers who were present for these tests decided to continue with their own experiments at Camp Evans. They planned to fly a recovered Japanese balloon, and began by checking reflectivity from the envelope itself. On 20 February 1945, the balloon was covered with a large net and inflated with approximately 10,000 cubic feet of helium. Moored to a winch attached to a truck, the balloon ascended to approximately 1,000 feet and after about an hour fell limp to the ground because of helium loss through the now weathered and porous paper.

In hope of continuing with the test, makeshift repairs were made for an attempted free-flight radar test path. Once again the balloon was inflated, this time with some 9,000 cubic feet of helium while still covered with the net for added envelope strength during the filling operation. Just prior to launch, an attempt was made to remove the net, but gusty surface winds were causing damage to the weakened skin. To prevent further damage, the balloon was released without valve or metal attachments. The balloon rose to approximately 4,500 feet and remained airborne for about thirty minutes before it finally settled into some trees about five and one-half miles away, damaged beyond repair.

A second balloon was acquired in much better condition—apparently never having been subjected to moisture—and on 28 February was inflated and released with the relief valve in place. It climbed to approximately 1,000 feet in free flight and was carried eastward by the wind. A navy "Texan" scout-trainer was assigned as escort and reference target for the radar evaluation. Should the balloon appear to endanger populated areas, the plane was to shoot it down. But because of poor visibility and wind speeds which reached seventy miles per hours, sight of the balloon was lost about ten miles out at sea. Thus ended the so-called laboratory testing of Japanese balloons, after little or no tangible results.

Figure 35. United States Navy personnel steady the ballast-dropping mechanism and bomb-carrying device. The main bomb is suspended in the center, while a ballast sandbag hangs at the right. (U.S. Navy photograph, 80-G-326354, in the National Archives)

Figure 36. On the left periphery of the release ring is a 5 kg thermite incendiary bomb sometimes used as ballast in the last release stations prior to the dropping of the main bomb. (U.S. Navy photograph, 80-G-326355, in the National Archives)

Other captive balloons had been inflated for inspection purposes. One of these was the much photographed balloon at Moffett Field, California. At the main West Coast antisubmarine base, the enormous blimp hangar provided excellent space for evaluating the balloon and its rigging.

A number of balloons were gathered for whatever purpose needed. One of these balloons that is in the National Air and Space Museum collection (accession number NASM 617) was recovered at Echo, Oregon, on 13 March 1945, after making the Pacific crossing (Figure 1). Military authorities at Walla Walla Army Air Base, Washington, sent the balloon to Moffet Field, California, which was a general collection center for these balloons. This balloon was transferred to the Smithsonian Institution by the War Department on 18 October 1945 from the Technical Air Intelligence Center, through the Naval Station Anacostia, D.C. Still another balloon (accession number NASM 2436) of little-known origin was received by the National Air and Space Museum from the NAS Lakehurst, New Jersey, on 7 June 1962. Presumably, this is the balloon which was sent to that station from NAS Moffett Field through NSC Oakland, 5 May (no year given) via the S.S. *Yugoslavian Victory,* marked: "Hold for National Air Museum."

Sunset Project

Detection and interception of the balloons was of continuing concern to Fourth Air Force. In order to arrive at the best defensive system, they initiated "Sunset Project" early in April 1945. This was to establish a test area covered by radar sites in an effort to detect actual Japanese balloons as they approached the Washington coast. This coverage extended from Cape Flattery in the north to the mouth of the Columbia River at the Oregon border. The locations and the types of equipment utilized were as follows:

Location	Search radar	GCI equipment
Paine Field	SCR-588-B	SCR-588-B
Cape Flattery	SCR-527*	SCR-584
Ruby Beach	SCR-271 (SCR-545)	SCR-545
Queets	SCR-527*	SCR-584
Raymond	SCR-588-B	SCR-588-B
Rochester	AN/TPS-1B	SCR-615-B

*The SCR-527 could not be used for GCI operation because of bad reflection and short range.

All of the equipment required for the project, however, was not immediately available to the Fourth Air Force. By the end of April, all but the SCR-584s had arrived at Paine Field and were ready for installation at the selected sites. The SCR-584 sets (which were used for ground-controlled interception) arrived early in May. Five of the search-radar units were in operation by 7 May, and the sixth set was placed in operation 18 May. By 8 June, all of the SCR-584 sets were in operation.

The operations of the project were to be of two types—search for balloons by radar, and interception by fighter planes guided by VHF ground equipment. Radar plots were to be reported to the Silver Lake Region Control Center where it was expected that balloon targets could be recognized by their speed, altitude, and relation to known wind currents. Intercept aircraft, such as P-38 "Lightnings" and P-61 "Black Widows," were to be kept on alert at Paine Army Air Field, Quillayute Naval Auxiliary Air Field, and Shelton Naval Auxiliary Air Field. Detailed weather information which would indicate the probable course of the balloons was to be furnished to the centrol group by the weather officer of the Fourth Air Force.

From reports of unusual signals from radio transmitters over the ocean, it was soon determined that these must be from approaching balloons. During the period from 6 December 1944 to mid-April 1945 when the offensive ended, ninety-five radio signals of the type believed to have been transmitted by balloons had been monitored. This, in effect, became the most positive form of alert, but it was not an aid to interception because so many balloons were without transmitters. Further, the signals would fade before they reached the coast. Because of technical problems, very few accurate tracks or plots to determine the origin of the signals had been obtained. From tracks that were plotted, it was evident that they followed the flow pattern of the winds over the sea at relatively the same speed. A direction-finder net was established to plot further signals.

Radio transmissions were generally of the same type: pulsed continuous wave signals of varying frequency and with marked transient characteristics. The pulse rates usually ranged from 20 to 150 pulses per minute. The frequencies usually ranged from about 5,000 kilocycles to over 12,000 kilocycles, with individual transmissions varying in some cases by more than 250 kilocycles.

As more plots and information became available, the Western Defense Command estimated the balloons were being released from the vicinity of Sendai, in the central east-coast region of the main island of Japan.

In further attempts to determine more closely the launching points of the balloons, military intelligence asked the United States Geological Survey to assist. Sand ballast samples from balloons found at Holy Cross, Alaska, and Glendo, Wyoming, were delivered to its chief mineralogist, Dr. Clarence S. Ross, in the hope that the place of origin might be determined. Several months went by while the samples were studied, and several

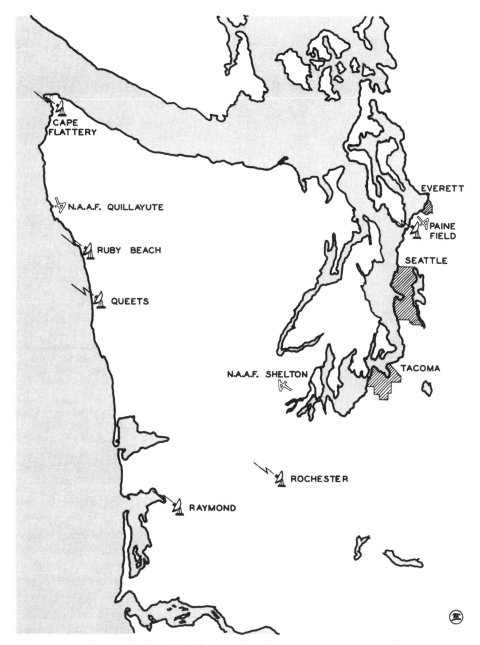

Figure 37. "Sunset Project" facility locations in the western portion of the state of Washington.

facts finally became evident. According to Dr. Ross, this was obviously beach sand, and the presence of fossils determined the northermost latitude along the Japanese seacoast from which this could come. The Geological Survey reported that the most likely source for both samples was the area in the vicinity of Shiogama on the east coast of Honshu, eight miles northeast of Sendai. The next most likely source was stated to be the beaches just south of Ohara, about forty miles southeast of Tokyo—this was Ichinomiya, an actual launch site. The samples showed slight variations such as would be expected in two samples collected from different parts of one beach (see Figure 16).

The Canadians were equally concerned about the balloon bombs and were performing similar tests with sand ballasts. In the samples they studied, their mineralogists had detected slag content which indicated sand from an area near a blast furnace. Close communication between the United States and Canada helped considerably to narrow down the launch sites.

Figure 38. Fighter-aircraft gun-camera film catches a balloon in flight. At the lower altitudes, the gas contracts which cavitates the lower portion of the sphere giving the impression of a parachute. (30771 AC)

Orders were dispatched for aerial reconnaissance coverage over selected areas of the eastern coastal areas where blast furnaces were known to have existed. A study of the aerial photographs taken on 25 May 1945 revealed what appeared to be partially inflated balloons in a barracks area and a possible release area near the beach. Three assembly plants were being built, two of which were connected by taxiways to an airfield adjacent to the city of Sendai. A large plant of the type usually found in a general arsenal were also seen, and it appeared to be the only heavily defended area in the vicinity. These findings were of little value, however, for the balloon offensive had already come to an end. Further, there was no postwar evidence of balloon launch sites having been located in this area near Sendai, leaving the question as to what had actually been photographed.

The balloon attacks had terminated by mid-April—before any of the units in the "Sunset Project" went into operation. The following statement of the results of the project is quoted from the report submitted to the Western Defense Command by the Fourth Air Force in August 1945.

> From the beginning of the project up to 8 June 1945, no radar detections or confirmed visual sighting had been observed or reported in the test area. In view of this lack of activity and of the fact that critical personnel was being used in the project, this Headquarters forwarded a letter to the Continental Air Force requesting manufacture or procurement of not less than twenty-five (25) flyable balloons of the Japanese type for use in the project, thus facilitating an early termination of the test. It was proposed to release these balloons at sea under favorable weather conditions which would bring them in over the coast ... CAF's reply to the above proposal was that it was not practical to provide these balloons. They further indicated that the project had decreased in importance in view of the Eleventh Air Force operational experience in balloon detection and destruction. In view of the CAF policy, this Headquarters initiated action to terminate the project ....

On 11 July 1945 Continental Air Force Headquarters granted authority to bring the project to an end, but it was not finally terminated until 1 August because of the necessity for obtaining similar approval from the Western Defense Command.

The results of the "Sunset Project" were practically zero. The project did not get under way until the Japanese had stopped launching. There were, therefore, no opportunities for the radar stations to detect any balloons and no chance for planes to shoot them down. Numerous reports of balloon sightings reached the Seattle Control Group, but practically all were identified as weather balloons, blimps, or the planet Venus, which was often mistaken for a balloon. Sixty-eight interceptions were attempted, but none was successful; the evidence indicates that these interceptions failed because the reports on the balloons were false alarms—there were no verified balloon sightings over the United States after the middle of April 1945. Thus, United States military operations against the balloon bomb came to an end.

Propaganda

With every new weapon system, the associated propaganda can often add to the overall effectiveness; however, because of American silence concerning this new threat, the Japanese were kept off balance in their propaganda program.

The silence was finally broken by the Japanese on 17 February 1945, in a Domei News Agency broadcast directed to the United States in English. The Japanese claimed that 500—some news accounts claimed 10,000—casualties had been inflicted in the United States and that numerous fires had been started. The broadcast also announced that the government authorities in the United States had found it necessary to issue general warnings about the attacks by the Japanese balloons and thus caused considerable alarm to the people. It was emphasized that these occurrences had shattered the American feelings of security against attacks by the Japanese.

This broadcast was the first of a series in a war of nerves against the United States. Subsequent Japanese broadcasts beamed to Europe, Southeast Asia, and China repeated this theme and, in one instance, added that several million airborne troops would be landed in the United States in the future.

These propaganda attempts brought no worldwide reaction. It was not until after the American broadcast to the public about possible dangers in tampering with these balloons and their apparatus, that the Japanese renewed their propaganda efforts. Following the United States warning to the public on 22 May 1945, a Domei radio broadcast from Lisbon, Portugal, on this same date and the day following, issued a paraphrasing of the American message.

A broadcast in English from Southern Domei News Agency in Singapore was recorded 4 June 1945. The broadcast was based on statements made at a press conference by Lieutenant Colonel Shozo Nakajima, a spokesman for Imperial Forces in the southern area, who had been associated with press and propaganda activities since August 1943. He reported that the balloons were causing havoc in the United States, even though thus far they had only been released on an experimental scale.

Nakajima also predicted that when the experimental period was over, "large-scale attacks with death-defying Japanese manning the balloons" would be launched. It was believed that the 32-foot balloon would be incapable of carrying a man from Japan to this continent with the necessary survival equipment at 30,000 feet; however, a balloon 62 feet in diameter—believed to be the largest practical size—could carry a useful load of about 2,600 pounds at 30,000 feet. According to the Army Air Forces' Material Division, such a balloon would require 1,350 pounds of ballast for a four-day trip. The minimum weight of a man with survival equipment (pressurized gondola, oxygen equipment, food, water, and clothing) was estimated to be 640 pounds. On the basis of this weight, it was believed possible to transport an agent from Japan to this country by a 62-foot balloon.

Japanese propagandists continued their efforts to inspire terror and divert forces in the United States. In addition, they tried to convince their Japanese audiences and others that the United States mainland had been successfully attacked with a new and ingenious weapon.

As a follow-up to the propaganda, Rikuro Shimuzu, a former press attaché of the Japanese Embassy in Argentina, and manager of the Domei News Agency in that country, stated that the bombing attack by balloons on the United States had produced more damage than the Americans had admitted. He said that the balloons were a "prelude to something big."

There was speculation as to what this "something big" might be. In some Japanese propaganda reports, there was the implication that this might be one-way suicidal attacks by long-range Japanese bombers. The Japanese were known to have types of planes which, if loaded with only the necessary fuel and bombs and flying with favorable winds, could make such a flight from Misawa Air Base and other bases in northern Honshu—to Seattle, or even to San Francisco.

A long-range bomber program was quite impractical, and no evidence indicated enemy agents were being transported by balloons. Through western eyes, the entire balloon program seemed impractical from the very start—yet, it was very much a fact. The content of any propaganda program could not be overlooked.

Conclusion

The "something big" referred to in Japanese propaganda messages, failed to materialize. The balloon offensive was terminated as suddenly as it had begun. Americans monitoring the program were puzzled by the cessation, for winds continued to be favorable for launchings, and the onslaught was absorbing United States military men and equipment in preparation for what might occur next.

The silence of the American public and self-censorship by the American press left the Japanese with considerable doubt as to the effectiveness of the Fu-Go Weapon. The attitude of the American people on the home front, and their cooperation with government officials for the good of the nation, was a major contribution toward ending these attacks.

If a lesson is to be learned from this history, it might be summarized best by an opening remark on the subject in a news release following the war:

> Japan was kept in the dark about the fate of the fantastic balloon bombs because Americans proved during the war they could keep their mouths shut. To their silence is credited the failure of the enemy's campaign.[10]

The Japanese had one thousand more balloons in readiness, but further launches were suspended in the early part of April 1945, primarily because the Showa Denko Company and other hydrogen sources were being disrupted by B-29 raids. Since the effectiveness of the program was uncertain to the Japanese, resources for these repairs were funneled to more urgent needs. Obviously, the "Fu-Go Weapon" was not the anticipated decisive weapon, but it was Japan's V-1 weapon in an effort to avenge Doolittle's April 1942 raid on Tokyo. Hardly more was attained than a psychological effort against the United States resulting in rumors and uncertainty, even though it was assumed that not more than ten percent ever reached the United States and Canada. Although some American publications printed statements that the Japanese army staff headquarters had ordered the balloon missions to be stopped, they were actually suspended because of the intensified United States air raids against Japan. With no report of their effect upon the North American continent, little effort was expended to make repairs after these raids. It was based upon these circumstances that the program was terminated.

From 4 November 1944 to 8 August 1945, 285 "incidents" were recorded, including 120 balloon recoveries; 32 balloon recoveries including bombs; 20 balloons downed but not recovered; 28 independent bomb incidents; and 85 related incidents.

In addition to the six Americans who were the only casualties in the United States as a result of foreign enemy action, the only recorded property damage was two small brush fires and the momentary loss of electrical power at the Hanford, Washington, atomic energy plant. Few were aware that one of these Japanese balloons caused a delay in the production of materials for the atomic bomb that would later be used on Japan. Elaborate safeguards were taken to prevent accidents in the reactor piles and uninterrupted cooling was essential. When the power was interrupted by the balloon, somewhere between Bonneville and Grand Coulee, it triggered the safety mechanism of the reactor. Since the system had never been tested, this incident gave everyone confidence in its safety although it necessitated three days of work to get the piles back to full capacity again.

The effort and expense by the Japanese in the balloon offensive was great in comparison to the minor results achieved. Balloons were reported over a very wide area of the North American continent stretching from the island of Attu to the state of Michigan, and from northern Alaska to northern Mexico.

The greatest weakness of the free balloon as a military weapon is that it cannot be controlled. The balloon campaign was an interesting experiment, but it was a military failure.

[10] *The New York Times*, 29 May 1947.

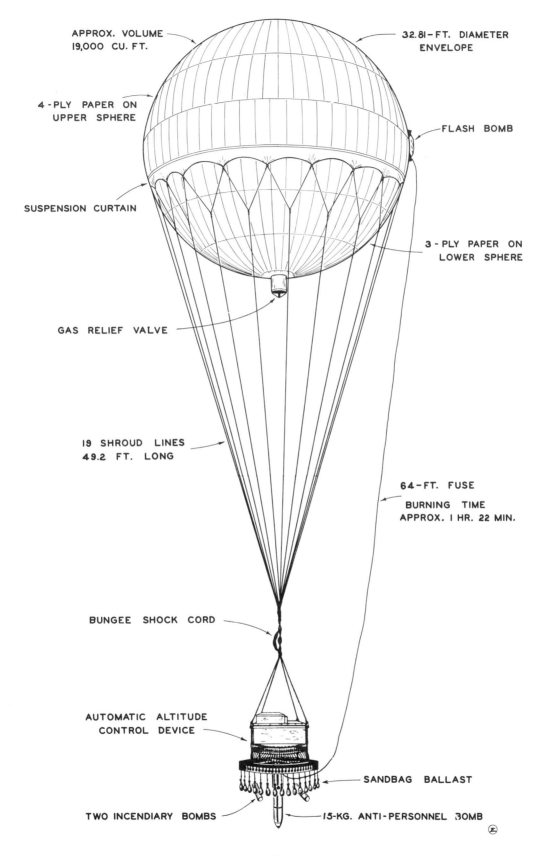

APPROX. VOLUME
19,000 CU. FT.

32.81-FT. DIAMETER
ENVELOPE

4-PLY PAPER ON
UPPER SPHERE

FLASH BOMB

SUSPENSION CURTAIN

3-PLY PAPER ON
LOWER SPHERE

GAS RELIEF VALVE

19 SHROUD LINES
49.2 FT. LONG

64-FT. FUSE
BURNING TIME
APPROX. 1 HR. 22 MIN.

BUNGEE SHOCK CORD

AUTOMATIC ALTITUDE
CONTROL DEVICE

SANDBAG BALLAST

TWO INCENDIARY BOMBS

15-KG. ANTI-PERSONNEL BOMB

Figure 39.   General arrangement of Japanese paper bombing balloon.

39

APPENDIXES

Detailed Description of A-Type Paper Balloon

Envelope

The balloon was a true sphere about 100 feet (32 meters) in circumference, 32.8 feet (10 meters) in diameter, and weighed about 152 pounds. When inflated, its volume approached 19,000 cubic feet.

The envelope was constructed from sections or gores of paper, varying from 38 to 64 in number. The paper color varied from pale greenish blue to yellowish white, and the final texture resembled varnished paper. A relief valve was attached to a circular opening at the bottom of the bag. A scalloped catenary skirt or band which encircled the envelope about 20 feet from the bottom, was 22 inches wide midway between the points. The points were four or five feet apart. The skirt was edged or bound with a continuous piece of rope which protruded at the point of each scallop, forming loops to which the shrouds were attached.

The material of the envelope consisted of four layers of thin, long-fiber paper cemented together with a hydrocellulose adhesive made from *konnyaku,* a common potato-like vegetable. When made into a paste or prepared for eating it is called *konnyaku-nori.* It was soluble in water and made up in proportions of one part adhesive stock and thirty-two parts water by weight. The layers of paper were laminated either by hand or machine. The machine method, although cheaper, yielded an inferior product. The laminated sheets of paper were dried in approximately thirty minutes by passing them through a dryer maintained at 70°C. The material then was dipped in a cleaning solution of soda-ash, washed in water, dried, and dipped in glycerine solution to increase pliability. This was necessary to keep the skin from cracking and hardening in the severe cold at high altitudes.

The cut patterns for each half of the spherical envelope were seamed over a form. This was followed by assembling the halves of the sphere and installing the remainder of the balloon parts.

The entire surface of the balloon was then coated with a waterproof lacquer, manufactured by the Nippon Paint Company, the composition of which, by weight, is as follows:

	Percent
Nitrocellulose	10
Triphenyl phosphate	5
Dibutyl phthalate	5
Benzol	25
Butyl acetate	10
Ethyl acetate	15
Acetone	10
Butyl alcohol	20
	100

The envelope was inflated with hydrogen, a highly inflammable gas. Assuming the balloon was filled to capacity with hydrogen, the net lifting power (buoyancy less weight of envelope) at various altitudes was as follows:

Altitude	Lifting power
Sea level	1033 lbs.
0.9 mi. (4,750 ft.)	876 lbs.
5.0 mil (26,400 ft.)	360 lbs.
6.8 mi. (35,900 ft.)	210 lbs.

Japanese engineering documents obtained after the war supported these findings, but the figures included the weight of the envelope:

Altitude	Lifting power
Sea level	360 kg. (794 lbs.)
10,000 m. (32,808 ft.)	184 kg. (406 lbs.)

Each balloon was pressure tested to seven inches of water for acceptance. About 10 percent of the hand-made balloons failed to meet these requirements. The percentage was even greater for the machine-made paper since this was a new process from the standpoint of fabrication and production. It was said that a rejected balloon when gas filled (1.97 inches water super pressure) lost sufficient gas in twenty minutes to effect a pressure reduction of 0.89 inches.

Findings from United States Tests on Paper Used for Envelope

The long-fiber paper gave high strength and the hydrocellulose provided adequate gas impermeability.

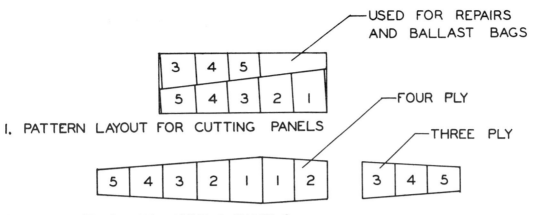

USED FOR REPAIRS
AND BALLAST BAGS

1. PATTERN LAYOUT FOR CUTTING PANELS

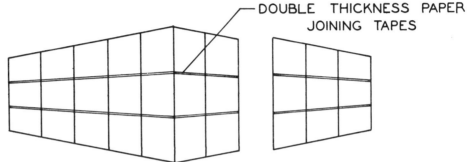

FOUR PLY

THREE PLY

2. LAMINATING AND JOINING PANELS

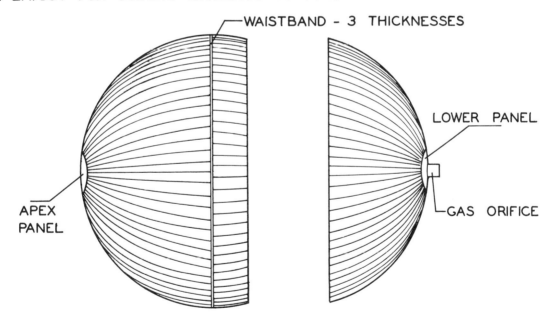

DOUBLE THICKNESS PAPER
JOINING TAPES

3. LAYOUT FOR JOINING SEGMENTS TO FORM SPHERE

WAISTBAND - 3 THICKNESSES

LOWER PANEL

APEX
PANEL

GAS ORIFICE

4. UPPER HEMISPHERE ASSEMBLY   5. LOWER HEMISPHERE ASSEMBLY

6. UPPER AND LOWER HEMISPHERES ARE JOINED BY INNER TAPE

7. ASSEMBLY IS COMPLETED BY WAISTBAND REINFORCING SEAM

Figure 40. Layout for cutting, pasting, and assembly of the balloon envelope.

The degradation of the cellulose to hydrocellulose was carried to the point that 20 percent of the total weight of the balloon material was water soluble. When wet, the material increased 67 percent in weight.

The tensile strength of the material when dry was 68 pounds per linear inch, and 37 pounds per inch when wet. The thickness ranged from .0075 to .009 inch. The weight of each ply was approximately 0.38 ounces per square yard. The balloon when inflated to a pressure of one ounce per square inch would be under a skin tension of six pounds per linear inch. A 1,000-pound weight hanging from the shroud lines would add an additional pound-per-linear-inch tension along the junction of the skirt with the envelope. The balloon was therefore amply strong enough to withstand an internal pressure of one ounce per square inch plus a load of 1,000 pounds.

The hydrogen permeability of the envelope material was 0.98 liters per square meter per day. This was about one tenth the permeability of the ordinary rubberized balloon fabric in use at that time. The rate of loss for the balloon was roughly 10 cubic feet per day, so in a week there was no significant decrease in lifting power owing to diffusion. The hydrogen permeability was determined on a 68-square-inch sample with hydrogen at one atmosphere on one side and air at one atmosphere on the other. The air was drawn past the membrane and its hydrogen content determined by analysis. A repetition of the experiment using one ounce of excess pressure on the hydrogen side gave the same permeability.

Relief Valve

The relief valve seat was pressed, .041-inch, sheet steel and consisted of a 19.5-inch-diameter cylindrical section cemented to the bottom of the envelope. Below the cylindrical section, the seat flanged inward and then down to form a second cylindrical section 16 inches in diameter and one inch high. The valve was a pressed-steel disc 17 inches in diameter covered with a thin rubber gasket and was forced against the valve seat by a compressed coil spring under adjustment tension. The coil spring was guided by an axial bolt through the valve sliding into a sleeve which was supported on three steel arms extending to the flange section of the valve seat where they were bolted.

This valve permitted gas to escape from the envelope when the gas expanded to a value of 0.06 pounds (one ounce) per square inch in the low pressure of high altitudes. Thus, the maximum altitude of the balloons was able to be limited.

Each valve was marked with large painted numbers.

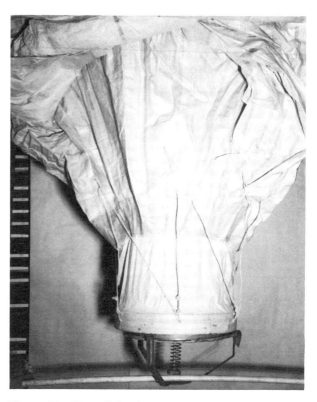

Figure 41. Gas relief valve glued in position at neck of envelope. This balloon was recovered near Holy Cross, Alberta, Canada, on 21 January 1945. (U.S. Army photograph, SC 237084)

Figure 42. The gas relief valve, nineteen and one-half inches in diameter, was spring-loaded against a one-ounce-per-square-inch gas pressure. This valve, marked with a chalk number "93," was recovered at Marshall, Alaska, 23 December 1944. U.S. Army photograph, SC 237090)

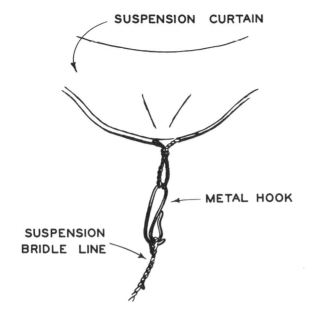

SUSPENSION CURTAIN

METAL HOOK

SUSPENSION BRIDLE LINE

At least two kinds of valves of the same type but slightly different in construction were used. Early valves were crowned for rigidity, while later ones were simply constructed of flat strap metal.

Shrouds

The 49-foot shroud lines were three-strand manila ropes, one inch in circumference. There were 19 such lines gathered together at the lower end in a double knot. A small pear-shape steel ring was tied into the lower knot. Each line branched by splicing into two lines about five feet from the upper end. There was a steel hook at each upper end for joining to the skirt of the balloon envelopes.

Fuses

Activating Fuses

Two fuses, 32½ feet long, were employed to activate the electrical circuits in the altitude-control apparatus when the balloon was launched. Burning time was approximately 54 minutes. These fuses were wound around the metal frame of the apparatus and terminated in two plugs in the upper metal ring. Either one of these fuses would complete the first electrical circuit action of the altitude-control apparatus.

Flash-Bomb Fuse

A 64¼-foot fuse ran from the bottom of the lower metal ring of the apparatus to the ignition charge, or flash bomb, on the side of the envelope. Burning time was 82 minutes.

Demolition-Block Fuse

A 26-inch fuse ran from the bottom of the lower metal ring of the apparatus to the demolition block on top of the apparatus.

Flash Bomb

The flash bomb or ignition charge which destroyed the envelope was attached to the envelope between its horizontal great circle and the catenary skirt or band. It consisted of 250 grams of magnesium flash powder in a paper container two inches wide by five inches long. It was cemented to the balloon. Its purpose was to destroy the balloon at the end of its mission. Later in the

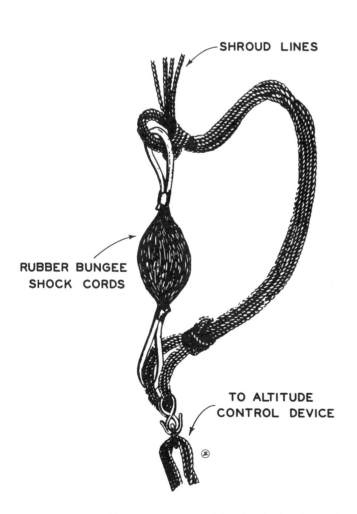

SHROUD LINES

RUBBER BUNGEE SHOCK CORDS

TO ALTITUDE CONTROL DEVICE

Figure 43. Flight-control, stanchion shock absorber and stanchion to balloon connection.

Figure 44. Timing fuses. (A72-872)

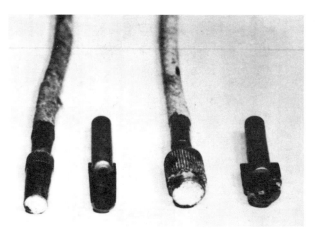

Figure 45. Fuse end connectors. (A72-872)

Figure 46. Though damaged by its use, this control frame was recovered near Marshall, Alaska, 23 December 1944. Note fuses circling frame. (U.S. Army photograph, SC 237091)

Figure 47. Demolition block, showing tin container and 2-pound, paper-covered, picric-acid charge. Holes on side and end are for blasting cap. (30777 AC)

operation, this flash charge was deleted from balloons. The reason has not been positively determined, but speculation dictates that by leaving the envelope intact at the end of its flight, there was greater chance of press reports of its arrival.

Shock Absorber

A 22-inch rubber rope with cotton-covered eyelets formed at each end was sometimes used as a shock absorber or bungee for the suspension of the apparatus from the shrouds. Eight strands of $^3/_8$-inch manila rope were knotted to both eyelets to form a sister which limited the elongation of the rubber rope. At the top end, the sister formed a loop carrying two open steel hoops which fastened through the pear-shape ring tied in the lower end of the shroud lines. At the bottom end, the sister was knotted about the lower end of the bungee, and then divided into four suspension cords of two rope strands each. The suspension cords were threaded through holes in each one of the four bolts at the top of the metal framework of the apparatus, with the cords passing back through the knots about the bungee to the top loops to give the sister its eight-strand strength. Measured load tests indicated that the shock absorber would be ineffective for loads in excess of 150 pounds. Some balloons did not have this bungee, but this did not alter the rest of the suspension assembly.

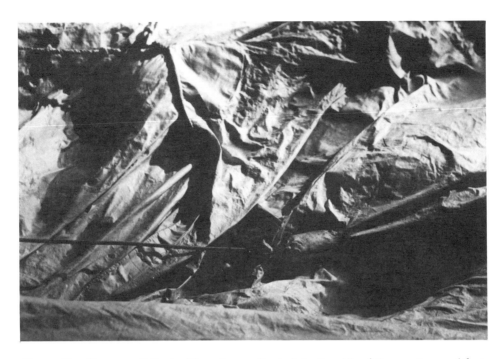

Figure 48. Close-up of the ignition charge attached to the side of the envelope and fuse leading to it. At the top left is a shroud line attached to the catenary band. (30781 AC)

Automatic Altitude-Control Device

A four-post metal frame approximately a foot square was suspended from the lower end of the bungee. In the center of the frame, there was a bakelite deck or panel which supported a box containing four barometric contractors. On top of this box, there was a wet-acid battery and a standard Japanese demolition block. Bolted to the bottom of the frame was a cast aluminum four-spoke wheel approximately 24 inches in diameter and 1½ inches thick, containing a system of fuses and black-powder charges that were activated by the barometric contractors or aneroids. These were designed so that when blown out, they released sandbags or other objects hung to the periphery of the wheel.

Just above and parallel to this wheel was an aluminum ring of smaller diameter containing holes for the other ends of the fuses, as well as an equal number of spring-tensioned switches.

Functions

The automatic altitude-control device had two functions: (a) to control the lower altitude limits, and (b) to release an object or objects carried by the balloon and then destroy the balloon and apparatus. These purposes were to be accomplished by the operation of aneroid-barometer (altimeter) elements, preset for the desired operational altitude, which caused ballasting increments

Figure 49. Ballast release and control frame. (A72-868)

and payloads to be dropped, and self-destruction charges to be set off.

Operation

A gas-filled balloon of this type could rise to maximum altitude during daylight hours when the gas inside the bag was warmed by the sun. During night hours, the gas cooled and contracted and the balloon

45

lost altitude. In order to prolong the flight of these balloons, a ballast-dropping mechanism was provided so that whenever a balloon descended to a predetermined minimum altitude, one or more "ballast objects" were dropped, thereby allowing the balloon to rise again. The ballast objects were sandbags hung around the periphery of the large metal ring at the bottom of the apparatus. In some cases incendiary and explosive bombs were attached in the same manner, indicating that ballast objects may have served a dual purpose.

The mechanism was initially activated after the balloon was high in the air, when the activating fuses, ignited on release, burned up to the upper metal ring of the apparatus causing two small plugs to blow out and release two spring-loaded contacts. This completed the electrical circuit of the apparatus except for the make-or-break contacts located in the aneroid barometers.

Three of the four aneroids were wired in parallel with each other. The fourth was a part of a separate electrical circuit. The three connected in parallel were arranged so that when a predetermined minimum altitude was reached, any one of the three could make a contact completing the electrical circuit. One of the aneroids was more carefully constructed than the others and was believed to be the primary control element, with the other two provided in case the primary element failed. When this electrical circuit was completed, two plugs located on the circumference of the large metal ring were blown out resulting in the dropping of the ballast they supported.

This blowout process also ignited two 24-inch squib fuses which served as a time delay of about two minutes

to allow the balloon to gain altitude before the next set of plugs fired. The firing of the next set of plugs—on the opposite side of the upper metal contact ring—closed spring-operated switches which again completed the electrical circuit of the apparatus except for the contacts at the aneroids. If the aneroid contacts were still closed at this time—by failure of the balloon to ascend sufficiently—another pair of blowout plugs located on the large metal ring was blown out and the process repeated. This process of dropping objects continued, alternating from one side of the large metal ring to another, until the balloon reached sufficient altitude to cause the aneroids' contacts to open and thus break the circuit. When the balloon later dropped to the minimum altitude, more ballast objects were caused to drop in the same manner.

An additional electrical circuit, connected to the fourth aneroid, was activated when the ninth set of blowout plugs on the upper contact ring had been fired. This circuit thereafter was completed at any time the fourth aneroid contact was closed, blowing out a plug under the large metal ring and igniting the fuse to the demolition charge on the top of the apparatus.

It was noted that any object or objects suspended by the two blowout plugs on the underside of the large ring would be released at any time the fourth aneroid closed its contact after the ninth set of plugs on the upper contact ring had been fired. Also, the mechanical apparatus would be destroyed at such time, before all of the ballast objects on the circumference of the large metal ring had been dropped, but the envelope could not be destroyed until the entire process was completed. The reason for this arrangement has not been determined.

Figure 50. Box cover containing aneroids is removed for viewing into the control device. (U.S. Army photograph, SC 226133)

Figure 51. Aneroids contained in a wooden container acted as the main control unit of the release mechanism. (U.S. Army photograph, SC 237087)

Figure 52. Bottom view of ballast-releasing control device. The ballast sandbags were mounted on the outer ring, while the main bomb was supported by the central shackle. (SC 226138)

Description of Components

Smaller Aneroid Barometers. The pressure element of the aneroids consisted of a small, flat, circular case constructed of thin, flexible metal—mostly brass—with concentric corrugation in the top and bottom. This pressure element collapsed gradually with increasing air pressure and returned to original size with decreasing pressure. In order to make this control the firing of blowout plugs, electric-circuit contacts were provided so that contact was made as the case collapsed. One electrical lead was fastened to a movable bar on which the pressure element was mounted. The other lead was attached to a straight wire which projected out over the pressure element. A small loop of wire attached to the top of the pressure element encircled this straight contact wire, and made contact with it, completing the electrical circuit; at this point, increasing air pressure made the case collapse. The element was adjustable by raising or lowering the movable bar by a thumb screw.

Central Aneroid Barometer

The operation of this aneroid was the same in general principle as that of the smaller aneroids. In this instrument, however, two pressure elements were used in series to permit greater accuracy of adjustment. It was used as the primary control unit and wired in parallel with two of the smaller aneroids.

Large Metal Ring

The purpose of the large metal ring was to suspend the ballast objects on its periphery and another object from the center of its underside. It had 72 equally spaced horizontal holes around its periphery, into which blowout plugs were fitted from the outside and from 70 of which, fuses extended on the inside. Fuses were not needed from the last pair of holes in the series. Five steel arming wires were attached to the ring; four on the periphery and one centrally located. These were used in connection with the bombs which frequently were suspended from the ring as dual-purpose ballast.

Attached to the top of the large metal ring were three fiber rings separated by two rows of electrical jacks with 72 jacks in each row. The lower row of jacks was wired in common while the upper row was wired in pairs. This arrangement allowed for two plugs in the large metal ring to be blown at the same time.

A wire from the inside of each pair of jacks located in the upper row was attached to the two corresponding connections on the bakelite plate. One lead from the lower row of jacks wired in common connected to the three aneroids wired in parallel, while another lead from this row of jacks connected to the plug centrally located under the large metal ring.

A lead from the outside of each jack in the upper and lower rows entered a corresponding blowout plug in the large metal ring to complete that portion of the electrical circuit.

The large metal ring was presumably made of aluminum or a light white-metal alloy. Four spokes at 90° angles, together with four metal suspension rods in vertical positions form the basis for support of the additional apparatus located above the ring.

Blowout Plug. The 70 blowout plugs located on the circumference of the large metal ring were small metal cylinders fitted tightly into the holes provided. The plugs contained a black-powder charge. As the electrical circuit to each plug was completed, the powder was ignited and exploded, blowing out the plug and causing the ballast object suspended by the plug to be released and dropped. This explosion also pulled corresponding small electrical plugs from jacks in the fiber rings and opened the circuits. The explosion additionally ignited the fuse which was attached to the inside end of the blowout plug. This fuse led to another blowout plug on the contactor ring above. The blowout plugs on the underside of the large metal ring operated in a similar

Figure 53. Aneroid board showing covers removed. These devices closed electrical circuits at pre-set minimum altitude for release of ballast. (A 37180E)

Figure 55. Fixed altitude aneroid for initial activation of the mechanism. (A72-869)

Figure 54. Aneroid board with covers in place. Japanese marked cover with triangle contains the aneroid that initially activated the electrical circuitry of the mechanism. (A 37180E)

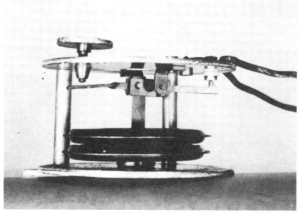

Figure 56. Master aneroid. Note thumb adjustment screw. (A72-869)

manner, but were wired separately and not as a pair; one ignited a fuse to the demolition block on the apparatus, while the other ignited a fuse to the flash bomb on the side of the envelope.

Both steel and aluminum die-stamped blowout plugs were used. Earlier varieties had been machined.

Switches on Upper Metal Contactor Ring. The switches which connected succeeding charges were located in the upper metal contactor ring and were operated by the explosion of a small blowout plug ignited by the fuse leading from the inside of the blowout plug on the periphery of the large metal ring below. The blowing out of this upper plug released a spring-actuated switch which made contact with clips on

(Continued on page 54)

Figure 57. This aneroid marked with a triangle on its cap rendered the altitude-control device inoperative until the balloon initially ascended through 6,000 to 16,000 feet. This served as a safety against inadvertent release of explosives. (72-870)

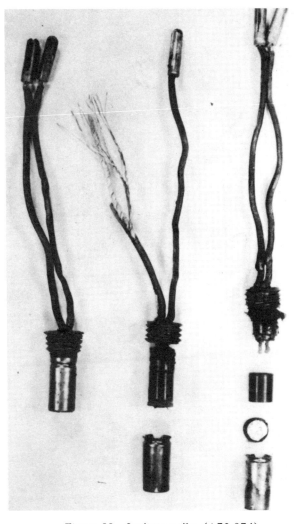

Figure 60. Blowout plugs, sectionalized. (A72-873)

Figure 58.. Igniter squibs. (A72-874)

Figure 61. Powder charge. (A72-873)

Figure 59. Blowout plugs and connecting fuses.
(72-876)

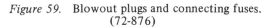

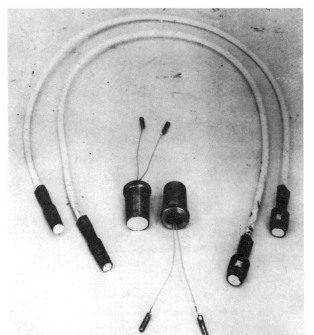

Figure 62. Main bomb-release shackle. When electrical power ignited blowout plugs (shown installed), fuses were also ignited—one for an explosive to destroy the apparatus, and another charge to explode the balloon. (72-875)

Figure 63. Main power supply was a single-cell, seven-plate, 2.3 volt, lead-acid storage battery. (72-871)

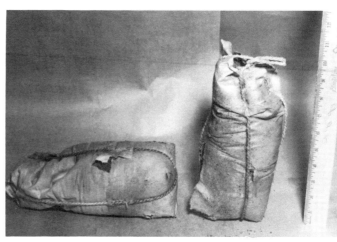

Figure 66. Thirty-two sandbags made up the ballast load for balloon altitude control. Individual weights were approximately seven pounds. (U.S. Army photograph, SC 237089)

Figure 64. Three parts of the double-walled, celluloid, battery box. Non-freeze liquid between walls helped control minimum temperature for continual battery output. (72-871)

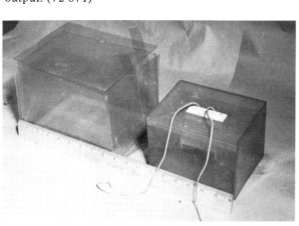

Figure 65. Battery box was constructed of clear celluloid to make full use of solar radiation to help sustain battery life. (U.S. Army photograph, SC 237096)

Figure 67. The bomb load and full ballast attached to a Japanese balloon gondola. Exploding blowout plug releases a sandbag shown in this movie still. The cycles continue, finally releasing the two incendiaries at left and the 33-pound, anti-personnel bomb which hangs nose down in the center. (29910 AC)

Balloon and apparatus as found
caught on a fence

Incendiary bomb found 75 feet
from balloon

Apparatus, showing number of fuses
not yet blown out

Apparatus caught on fence

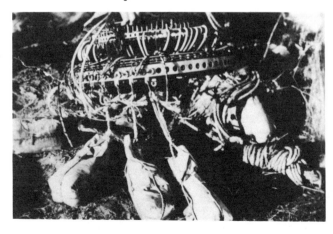

Close-up of gondola with
sandbags attached

Top of device showing aneroid
control board

Figure 68.   On-scene, balloon-recovery pictures taken 13 March 1945. (30772 AC)

Figure 69. Minutely detailed, exploded-view drawing prepared in 1945 shows the workings of the ballast and ordnance-dropping mechanism. (A 37180D)

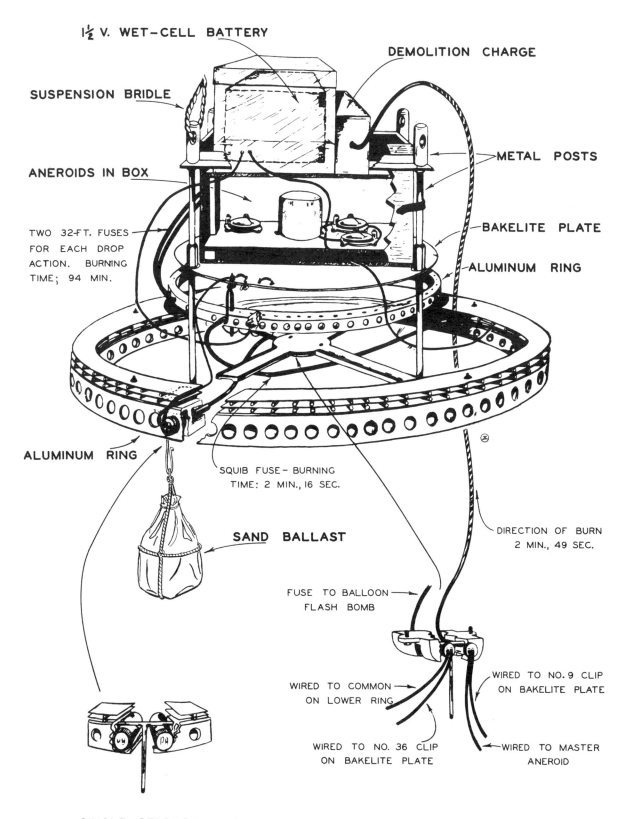

1½ V. WET-CELL BATTERY

DEMOLITION CHARGE

SUSPENSION BRIDLE

METAL POSTS

ANEROIDS IN BOX

BAKELITE PLATE

ALUMINUM RING

TWO 32-FT. FUSES
FOR EACH DROP
ACTION. BURNING
TIME; 94 MIN.

ALUMINUM RING

SQUIB FUSE — BURNING
TIME: 2 MIN., 16 SEC.

SAND BALLAST

DIRECTION OF BURN
2 MIN., 49 SEC.

FUSE TO BALLOON
FLASH BOMB

WIRED TO NO. 9 CLIP
ON BAKELITE PLATE

WIRED TO COMMON
ON LOWER RING

WIRED TO NO. 36 CLIP
ON BAKELITE PLATE

WIRED TO MASTER
ANEROID

SINGLE RELEASE UNIT

ONE "T" BAR, TWO BLOWOUT PLUGS

CENTER MAIN
BOMB RELEASE

Figure 70. Automatic altitude-control device.

(Continued from page 48)
the bakelite panel. The contact clips were wired in pairs which would operate even if one circuit failed.

Bakelite Panel Contacts. Immediately above this ring of switches was a circular bakelite panel carrying a contact for each switch. Each single lead from the bakelite panel led down one of the adjacent vertical frame rods and connected to a pair of jacks wired in parallel in the fiber rings directly above the large metal ring. The bottom of each switch was wired in common to the battery. The other lead from the battery went through the aneroid control and via a common wire back to the dropping plugs in the large metal ring below. Thus, each switch or pair of switches armed one dropping circuit which would fire a pair of dropping plugs when the aneroid contacts closed.

Battery. The battery that supplied the current to fire the various blowout plugs was located in a large transparent container mounted on top of the control mechanism. The container was made of clear plastic material and double-walled with about an inch of air space between the inner and outer walls, to insulate the battery from the cold of high altitudes and obtain more effect from the heating provided by sunlight during the day.

The battery was a small, wet-cell type having five plates and measured 2½ by 3 by 1¼ inches. It was filled with a 10 percent solution of calcium chloride. This solution would tend to hold the battery between $0°$ and $-20°C$ until the solution would freeze solid at extreme altitudes.

This description from United States technical reports varies to some degree in the solution to antifreeze battery development in Japanese reports. They describe the final result as a liquid cell with sulphuric acid. Each cell was protected from cooling by covering it with a layer of nonfreezing liquid on all sides and placed in a heat-insulating, double case made of celluloid.

Ballast

On the average the ballast for the balloon consisted of 32 sand-filled paper bags, together with some bombs. The sandbags were made of the same material as the envelope and were usually bound with twine. The filled bags varied in weight from three to seven pounds and the total ballast weight was about 155 pounds. Both the bags and the bombs were suspended by "T" lugs inserted into slots in the bottom of the large metal ring, with each wing of the lug resting upon one of the blowout plugs in the ring. When either of the plugs was blown out, the lug fell by gravity from the slot.

Demolition Charge

The demolition charge carried for the purpose of destroying the mechanism was a two-pound block of picric acid wrapped with waxed paper and sealed in a tinned box 2½ by 3 by 6 inches. Connected to the mechanism was a short length of safety fuse to which was fastened a non-electric blasting cap inserted in one of the demolition charges.

B-Type Rubberized-silk Balloon

The navy-originated balloon consisted of gum-coated, *habutae*-silk,[1] laminated panels. Four layers formed the top half of the sphere while three layers formed the bottom half. Geometry of design was similar to the A-Type balloon, but was one meter less in diameter. Each connecting part was sewed together with a 40 millimeter seam which was sealed with cotton tape. After the balloon was inflated and tested, leaks were sealed with a benzol-gum concentrate.[2] These coatings on the silk gave the balloon a dark grey, rubber-like appearance.

This balloon also carried an automatic ballast-release system to compensate for inherent gas leakage, although it was not as complicated as the A-Type balloon system. The unit carried 14 ballast sandbags that were normally expended after four descending cycles that were detected by four aneroids and a simple release system.

Both military establishments and industry manufactured the A-Type balloon, while the B-Type rubberized-silk balloons were made only by private industry. Apparently no serious production problems were encountered with this more durably constructed balloon.

---

[1] Rated tensile strength of 67 pounds per square inch.
[2] United States test results made upon a retrieved B-Type balloon indicated that gas loss through the envelope was approximately 350 cubic feet per day.

Physical and Performance Characteristics of the Two Types of Balloons

	A-Type paper	B-Type silk
Volume, cubic feet (maximum)	18,600	13,450
Diameter of envelope (feet)	32.81	29.53
Length of foot ropes (feet)	49.20	No Data
Gas valve, diameter (inches)	15.76	9.85
valve setting (in H_2O)	1.97	21.50
Weights, balloon without equipment (pounds)	132 to 176	355
equipment (pounds) (flight control)	44	18
ballast (pounds)	198	97
bombs (pounds)	77	60
Total weight (pounds)	451 to 495	*530
Gas volume for flight (cubic feet)	7580	8000
Unit lift of gas (pound/cubic feet)	0.0687	0.0687
Gross lift (approx. pounds)	520	550
Free lift (approx. pounds)	24 to 65	*20
Rate of ascent with 65-pound free lift (feet/minute)	780	No Data
Gas volume/total volume	0.407	0.595
Computed altitude to height of fullness (approx. feet)	27,600	16,700

*Estimated

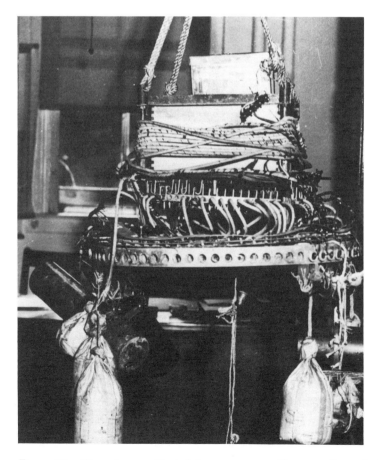

Figure 71. Though complicated in appearance, the operating principle of the altitude-control system was quite simple. Time burning fuses encircle the aneroid-containing box which supports the battery box above. (U.S. Army photograph, SC 226136)

Figure 72. Numbered holes containing blowout plugs for releasing sand ballast and bombs were designed to operate in pairs. The failure of any one did not hamper the sequence of the release or timing mechanism. (A 37180A)

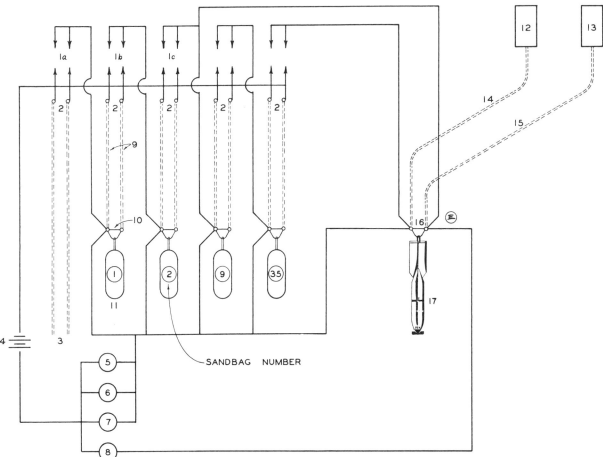

Figure 73. Schematic diagram of altitude-control apparatus for a paper bombing balloon.

1a. Trigger switch. When closed it sets up circuit for first bag of ballast.

1b,1c, etc. Trigger switches. When closed, they set up circuit for each preceding bag of ballast.

2. Trigger-switch plug. When blown from frame by charge of powder it closed trigger switch 1a, 1b, etc.

3. Long fuse. This fuse was ignited when balloon was launched. The fuse ignited trigger-switch plug (2).

4. Battery. To furnish current to trigger-switch plug (2) and blowout plugs (10) to release bags of ballast.

5 and 6. Barometric switches.

7. Barometric switch closed circuit for discharging ballast bags whenever balloon descended a distance below the pressure height of the balloon to a pressure increase of 700 mm.

8. Time switch set to close circuit for blowout plug (11), 60 to 70 hours after the balloon was launched.

9. Fuses to ignite trigger-switch plug (2) and cause trigger switch to close.

10. Connection containing blowout plugs to release ballast bag (11) and ignite fuse (9).

11. Ballast bag. Weight approximately 6.6 pounds.

12. Charge located on envelope to ignite and destroy balloon.

13. Charge to destroy flight-control apparatus.

14 and 15. Long fuse.

16. Connection containing blowout plug to release bombs and ignite fuses (14) and (15).

17. Bombs.

Hopper-Type Flight-control Apparatus

An additional ballast-dropping device was developed by the Japanese for altitude control. This was the Hopper Type, but used only on A-Type balloons, and in very small quantities. This system was equally as unique as the first and therefore worth recording.

It consisted of two main parts; a hopper-bottom storage bin capable of carrying 265 pounds of sand

ballast and a metering devise to release ballast in 5.5 to 6.5-pound increments. When the balloon descended a distance equivalent to a 700-millimeter increase in barometric pressure, a barometric switch closed and an electric circuit thus started the ballast-metering device. This, in turn, released the ballast increments at two to three-minute intervals until the balloon again ascended sufficiently to open the electric circuit.

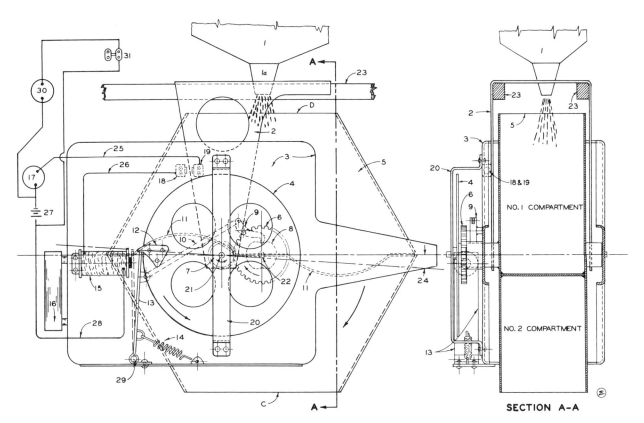

Figure 74. Schematic diagram of ballast-dispensing apparatus for Hopper-Type flight-control unit.

1. Sand storage bin
1a. Funnel
2. Bracket to support (3)
3. Housing
4. Disc, attached to gear (7)
5. Ballast dispensing container
6. Gear attached to (5) and in mesh with (7)
7. Gear. See 4 and 6
8. Cam, an integral part of (6)
9. Rocker, hinged at (30) which is hinged to (3)
10. Lever connecting (13) and (9)
11. Diaphragm dividing (5) into two compartments
12. Stop attached to (4)
13. Trip lever
14. Spring to keep (13) against stop (12)
15. Electric magnet

16. Counterweight
17. Two barometric switches
18 and 19. Contact points of circuit switch
20. Bracket for (21)
21. Shaft about which (3) rotates
22. Shaft about which (5) rotates
23. Support for (2)
24. The angle of housing (3) can take when (18) and (19) have made contact
25, 26, and 28. Conductors of the electric circuit
27. Battery
29. Hinge pin for (13)
30. Time switch, set to close the circuit 60 to 70 hours after the balloon was launched
31. Fuse plugs to release bombs and ignite long fuses to charges for destroying balloon and equipment

Ballast Metering Device

A schematic diagram of the ballast metering device is shown on page 57. The rotating container (5) was used to dispense small increments of ballast whenever required. A partition (11) divided the container into two compartments, each holding 5.5 to 6.5 pounds of sand. Gear (6), cam (8), and shaft (22) were integral parts of the container, and the entire sub-assembly rotated clockwise in the housing (3). The container (5) being empty, the housing (3) and component parts assumed the position shown in the diagram. This was accomplished by a counterweight (16) and a stop between the housing (3) and the frame (2). The center of gravity of the unit was located slightly to the left of the shaft (21); however, as the container (5) was filled with sand from the hopper, the center of gravity of the parts referred to above moved to a position to the right of the shaft (21) causing the housing (3) and parts attached thereto to tip and assume an angle (24) and, in turn, close the contacts between switch points (18 and 19). These switch points also acted as a stop, limiting the angle (24). The center of gravity of the container (5) full of sand was located to the right of the shaft (22). The container was prevented from rotating by the engagement of stop (12) against trip lever (13), the former having positive engagement with the disc (4) and gears (7) and (6). The container of sand now was in readiness to be dumped.

The element (17) consisted of two switches in series, one (17a) of which kept the electric circuit open until the balloon attained an altitude above the height at which the ballast was dropped. When it closed, it remained locked in this position for the duration of the flight. The other switch (17b) closed the circuit whenever the balloon descended a distance below the pressure height of the balloon or the height of stable flight, equivalent to a 700-millimeter increase in barometric pressure.

Let it be assumed that the balloon was descending and switch (17b) closed the circuit. At this instant, the magnet (15), energized by the battery (27), forced the trip lever (13) to the position indicated. The disc (4), connected to gear (7) in mesh with gear (6), was free to rotate allowing container (5) to revolve 180° dumping its contents as ballast. During this operation the disc rotated 360°, the housing (3) tilted back to a neutral position, opening the circuit at switch points (18) and (19) and trip lever (13) returned to normal position locking the container in position with stop (12) and cam (8). Two to three minutes were required to refill the container. As soon as this occurred, the housing (3) tilted to angle (24), closing the switch points (18 and 19).

If the switch (17b) was still closed, the second increment of ballast was dumped. This operation continued until the balloon ascended to an altitude sufficient to open the barometric switch (17b). A time switch (31), closed the circuit to the fuse plugs (32) 60 to 70 hours after launching, igniting the long fuses leading to the explosive charges to destroy the apparatus and burn the balloon.

Payload Ordnance

Two types of incendiary bombs and one type of high-explosive bomb were reported to have been carried as balloon payloads. Data concerning these bombs are extracted from the postwar-issued United States Air Force T/O 39B-1A-11, *Japanese Explosive Ordnance,* GPO 1953. This varies in some minor degree with information published in balloon-bomb reports while the operation was in progress.

5-kg. Thermite Incendiary Bomb

Fuses: Mechanical impact tail fuse
Overall length: $15^3/_4$ inches
Length of body: $6^3/_4$ inches
Diameter of body: $3^{11}/_{16}$ inches
Thickness of wall: $^1/_8$ inch
Material of wall: Welded steel tube
Type of suspension: Horizontal
Suspension lug: $^3/_4$-inch steel band secured around the body by a nut and bolt, $^5/_{16}$-inch hole drilled in the extension of the band to accept metal hook
Color and marking: Bomb body, black or olive drab; tail unpainted tin color
Length of tail: 9 inches
Width of tail: $3^{11}/_{16}$ inches
Width of tail fins: None
Dimensions of tail struts: None
Material of tail: Tin-plated sheet steel
Type of filling: Incendiary, consisting of a first fire charge and a main charge
Total weight of bomb: 11 pounds

Construction of Body

The bomb body consists of a $^1/_8$-inch-thick steel tube welded longitudinally and closed at the forward end by a 3.4-inch-thick nose plug which is welded in place. A cylindrical wooden block is fitted part way into the aft end of the body and secured by six countersunk wooden screws. The block contains the simple impact fuse and spring-loaded safety pin and also acts as the connecting element between the body and the tail. Two $^3/_8$-inch vent holes are drilled longitudinally through the block, 180° apart. The fuse is $2^7/_8$ inches long and has a $1^3/_{16}$-inch diameter. A tubular aluminum body contains a striker and a creep spring. A solid threaded plug closes the aft end and a plug containing the primer screws into the forward end. A spring-loaded safety pin holds the striker in position. The incendiary filling in the bomb body consists of a first fire charge which is adjacent to the primer and a main charge below the first fire charge. The first fire charge is a compressed black powder composed of magnesium, barium peroxide, and potassium nitrate. The main charge is thermite.

Construction of Tail

The tail, consisting of a tinned sheet-steel tube closed at the after end, is secured to the wooden block by five wooden screws. The tail and body sections rest flush against one another, completely concealing the wooden block to which they are attached. A slot in the tail receives the brass safety pin housing which is contained in the wooden block.

Operation

When the bomb is released the arming wire is withdrawn, allowing the spring-loaded safety pin to fly out, arming the fuse. On impact, the striker compresses the creep spring and hits the primer. The explosion of the primer ignites the first fire charge and the thermite.

Type 97 12-kg. Thermite Incendiary Bomb

Fuses: A-2 (a) (fitted with a magazine)
Overall length: 25½ inches
Length of body: 14½ inches
Diameter of body: 4 inches
Thickness of wall: $^3/_{16}$ inch
Material of wall: Steel
Type of suspension: Horizontal
Suspension lug: Normal army suspension lug on barrel, plus an improvised suspension device described below

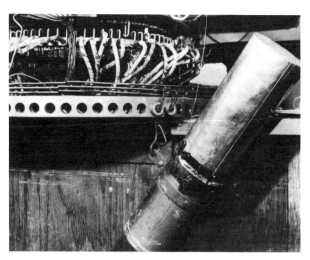

Figure 75. Eleven-pound incendiary bombs were often used in the final ballast-dropping positions on the periphery of the mechanism. (U.S. Army photograph, SC 226134)

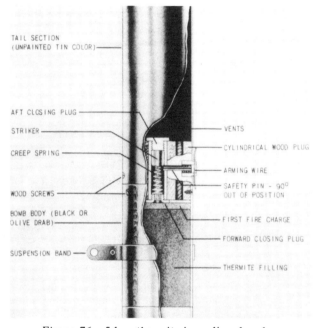

Figure 76. 5-kg., thermite incendiary bomb.

Figure 77. Exploded view of a 26-pound incendiary bomb found near Hayfork, California, 1 February 1945.

Color and markings: Black overall with a $^9/_{16}$-inch white
   stripe just forward of the suspension lug
Length of tail: 11 inches
Width of tail: $5^7/_{16}$ inches
Width of tail fins: $2^3/_{16}$ inches
Dimensions of tail struts: Length, $3^7/_8$ inches; width,
   $^3/_8$ inch; thickness, $^1/_{16}$ inch
Material of tail: $^1/_{16}$-inch rolled steel
Type of filling: Three thermite-filled magnesium fire
   pots; two black-powder charges
Weight of filling: Fire pots, 10 pounds; black-powder
   charges, 11 ounces
Total weight of bomb: 26 pounds
Charge/weight ratio: 38 percent

Construction of Body

A cast-steel nosepiece is screwed into a tubular-steel
body. A normal, hinged, army suspension lug and an
additional suspension device are fitted to the body. The
suspension device consists of two steel bands, $^{11}/_{16}$ inch
wide, each secured around the body by a bolt and nut.
The bands are joined by a ½-inch-wide steel strip which
is welded to them. A ¼-inch steel rod formed into a
suspension yoke is welded to the steel strip. A tail cone
is welded to a collar which fits into the aft end of the
body and is held in place by four rivets.

Construction of Tail

Four steel fins are welded to the tail cone and are
braced by a single row of box-type struts.

Operation

The fuse is armed in flight and on impact the
magazine is fired which, in turn, ignites the black-
powder charge. The flash from this charge travels down a
central flash channel igniting the incendiary composition
in the fire pots and firing the black-powder charge in the
tail. The explosive force of the two black-powder
charges is sufficient to shear the four rivets at the aft end
of the bomb body and thus expel the fire pots.

Remarks

The suspension yoke will be found on this bomb only
when it is suspended from a balloon.

Type 92 15-kg. High-explosive Bomb

Fuses: A-2 (b), A-2 (d)
Overall length: 25½ inches
Length of body: 14½ inches

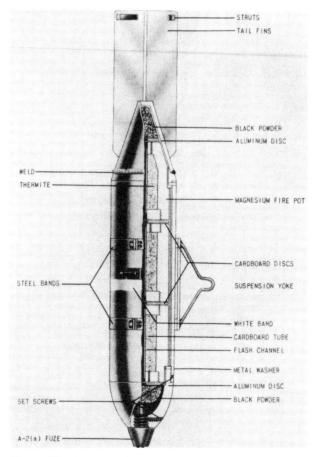

Figure 78. Type 97, 12-kg., thermite incendiary bomb.

Figure 79. This 33-pound anti-personnel bomb was
usually the main weapon carried on the central shackle
of the release mechanism. (U.S. Army photograph, SC
226137)

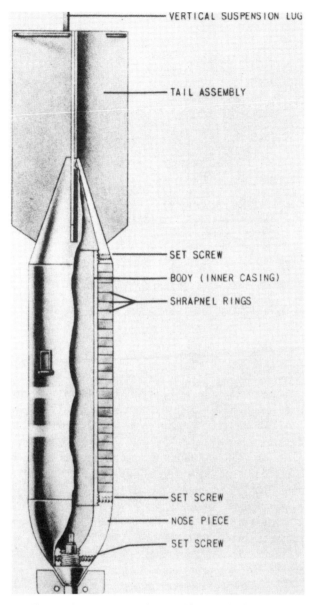

VERTICAL SUSPENSION LUG

TAIL ASSEMBLY

SET SCREW

BODY (INNER CASING)

SHRAPNEL RINGS

SET SCREW

NOSE PIECE

SET SCREW

Figure 80. Type 92, 15-kg., high-explosive bomb.

Diameter of body: $3^7/_8$ inches

Thickness of wall: ½ inch

Material of wall: Steel rings (26).

Type of suspension: Vertical and horizontal

Suspension lug: Normal army suspension lug. Rectangular, hinged, steel lug on a plate riveted to the body with four rivets. A similar steel-hinged lug is fastened to end of tail fins

Color and markings: Black overall with red band around the nose and a white band and yellow band forward of the suspension lug. (White band may be missing)

Length of tail: 11 inches

Width of tail: 5½ inches

Width of tail fins: $2^3/_4$ inches

Dimensions of tail struts: Length, $3^3/_4$ inches; width, $5/_{15}$ inch; thickness, $1/_{16}$ inch

Material of tail: $1/_{16}$-inch sheet steel

Type of filling: 3 precast blocks of picric acid. An alternative filling is cast TNT

Weight of filling: 9 pounds 9 ounces

Total weight of bomb: 33 pounds

Charge/weight ratio: 30 percent

Construction of Body

A cast-steel nose is threaded onto a tubular steel body. Twenty-six steel rings $3/_8$-inch wide and $3/_8$-inch thick are fitted around the body. One ring to which the suspension lug is attached is $1^3/_8$-inch wide and $3/_8$-inch thick. A tail cone is screwed onto the aft end of the tubular body.

Construction of tail: Four angular fins are welded to the tail cone and braced by a single set of box-type struts. A suspension lug is secured to the aft end of the fins.

Balloon Production

Pertinent data regarding the production of both types of balloons are tabulated below. The cost indicated does not include the flight-control apparatus.

The study of mass producing the paper skin, that otherwise was handmade, began in May 1944. After establishing a provisional production process by the end of July, army personnel gave first-hand instruction in the workshops on a rotation basis. Some did not receive this training until August. By October, all workshops were

trained and under the control of the Army Arsenal and were ordered to begin making the paper balloons on a rigid production schedule. This continued for five months that ended in February 1945. The production of 10,000 balloons was a vast undertaking, requiring millions of people.

As one example of production, the Iwahana factory of the arsenal completed about 700 balloons for the period of five months with 400 employees of the factory

Manufacturer	Production		Number procured	Cost each in yen[a]
	Started	Stopped		
Paper balloons:	1944	1945	3,000	10,000
Chugai Kako K.K.	1 April	15 February	3,693	5,500
Kokusan Kagaku Kogyo	September	March		
Sagami Arsenal ⎫				
Osako Arsenal ⎬ - - - - - - - - - - - - - - - - - - - no data - - - - - - - - - - - - - - - - - - -				
Kudura Arsenal ⎭				
Rubberized-silk balloons:				
Fugikwia Kogyo Corp.	September	April	50 to 60[b]	
Kokka Kogyo K.K.	October 1943	15 March	36[c]	3,350[d]

[a]The prewar exchange rate was five yen to the dollar. The post-hostilities rate was stabilized at fifteen to the dollar.

[b]Twenty to thirty of these balloons built between September 1944 and February 1945 were experimental and were said to have been flown. The twenty to thirty production models were destroyed by bombing.

[c]Eight to ten of these balloons were experimental, built between October 1943 and October 1945. No data are available as to whether they were flown.

[d]This cost did not include the silk cloth, used in the envelope fabric, which was furnished by the army.

---

and the students from nine girls' high schools in Gunma Prefecture participating in the work. The cutting and pasting of the thin sheets of paper were more skillfully done by females than by males.

Hydrogen Supply

Although the amount of hydrogen required to fill one balloon was only 27 kg., the transportation of this essential gas to the launch sites was a major undertaking. Because of these inherent difficulties, this was responsible for the slow beginning of the balloon offensive.

Hydrogen was compressed at the generating plant to a pressure of 150 atm. and put into 6,000 l. cylinders for transportation. Although the amount required to inflate one balloon was 300 m.^{3}, about 52 cylinders on the average were used per balloon. This amount included what was lost by balloon leakage during the inflation operation. Since the weight of one container was a little more than 133 pounds, transportation of 3.2 tons of metal containers were required for each balloon.

In March 1945, when about 3,000 balloons were released, more than 80 tons of hydrogen were consumed. Thousands of tons of metal containers were needed for transporting the hydrogen.

The following table is an indication of the vastness of this requirement for the balloon operation.

Frequency*	Balloons released	Hydrogen required in (N.T.P.)m^3	Number of cylinders	Cylinder weights in tons
1 balloon	1	300	52	3.2
1 release point (per day)	6	1,800	312	19.2
1 battalion (per day).	30	9,000	1,560	96
3 battalions (per day)	100	30,000	3,120	187
Monthly requirement	2,000	600,000	37,440	2,226
Total balloons released	9,300	2,790,000	295,600	17,760
Total balloons planned to be released	10,000	3,000,000	312,000	18,720

*Days during a month favorable for the release of balloons were about 20. Hydrogen for 3 battalions and cylinders for 2 battalions were available.

Of the 80 tons of hydrogen programmed, 50 tons were to be compressed into 97,500 cylinders and transported to Nakoso and Ichinomiya, while the remaining 30 tons were piped directly to the launch pads at Otsu. Considering the refueling of the gas cylinders, 20,000 would be needed; however, by late December—well into the launch program—only 8,000 cylinders were on hand. Consequently, the number of balloons released in November and December fell considerably short of what had been programmed. Though release of 150 balloons a day was the combined schedule for the three launch sites, about 30 was the actual figure.

A rapid shuttle system of empty and filled hydrogen tanks could have met the demand, but the frequent air raids against the rail lines immensely hampered the transportation of the gas.

The 1st Battalion at Otsu utilized hydrogen that was generated from caustic soda and ferrosilicon in the following formula.

$$2NaOH + Si + H_2O = Na_2SiO_3 + 2H_2$$

This required more than 2,000 tons of caustic soda to launch 4,000 balloons. The requirement of ferrosilicon was in the same proportion required by the formula—no small amount.

Fire was an ever-present danger and not an uncommon occurrence at the launch site. Hydrogen mixed with oxygen became highly inflammable, and was even more dangerous when heated during the transfer operation while filling the balloon. Attached to the base of the balloon was a paper-made, 50-centimeter-radius hose—20 to 30 meters in length—connected to the rubber hose which led to the gas-supply chamber. This rubber hose could be crimped off quickly at the first sign of fire. Men with buckets of sand were always poised to extinguish the first flicker of fire, while others would quickly turn off all of the gas valves. Stock piles of incendiary and high-explosive bombs, paper balloon envelopes, and hydrogen tanks provided a constant threat of fire and destruction at the launch sites.

Inflating and Launching

The methods used by the Japanese to inflate and launch the A-Type and B-Type bombing balloons were, for all practical purposes, similar. The discussion which follows applies particularly to the A-Type (paper) balloon.

An inflation bed was prepared by sinking 19 screw anchors into the ground as shown in Figure 81. This was followed by laying out the balloon within the screw-anchor circle, connecting the inflation tube to the inflation appendix, and securing the suspension bridles to the open eye of the screw anchors. The inflation equipment—including inflation tubing and manifold with high-pressure hose—were the same as those used for barrage balloons. Two cylinders were emptied at a time. Approximately 8,100 cubic feet of hydrogen were required for inflation and launching. The method used to determine the amount of gas supplied to the balloon is shown in Figure 81. Approximately 860 pounds of buoyancy was attained before release.

After removing the inflation tubing from the balloon, the gas valve was installed. Long ropes with an eye were reeved through each loop provided in the suspension curtain and hooked to the eye in the screw anchor. The suspension bridle was then removed. During this operation, one crewman alongside held the balloon in the position shown in Figure 81. Following this, the equipment was installed and the balloon allowed to rise until the equipment cleared the ground. The instruments and other equipment were checked and half of the long ropes were removed from the balloon. The long fuses were ignited, followed by unhooking the long ropes from the screw anchors and the balloon was released. The crewmen held onto one end of the long ropes. If the rope moved easily through the loop in the suspension band, it was recovered; if it became entangled, it was released and allowed to ascend with the balloon. This method of launching was used only when the surface wind was mild.

When the wind exceeded two and one-half miles per hour another method of launching was employed. The balloon was inflated in the same manner as previously described. Instead of using long ropes to raise the balloon in order to suspend the equipment, the balloon was held in position close to the ground until it was launched. A launching sandbag arrangement, as illustrated in Figure 82, was secured to alternate suspension points on the balloon and corresponding screw anchors on the ground. The equipment was suspended from a tilting arm on a wooden stand as shown in Figure 82.

At a given signal, the balloon was released from the screw anchors. It ascended, carrying with it the paper

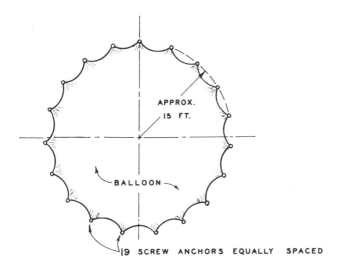

APPROX.
15 FT.

← BALLOON →

19 SCREW ANCHORS EQUALLY SPACED

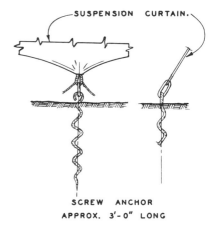

SUSPENSION CURTAIN.

SCREW ANCHOR
APPROX. 3'-0" LONG

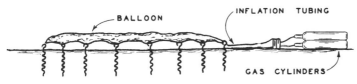

BALLOON

INFLATION TUBING

GAS CYLINDERS

LAYOUT OF BALLOON
FOR INFLATION

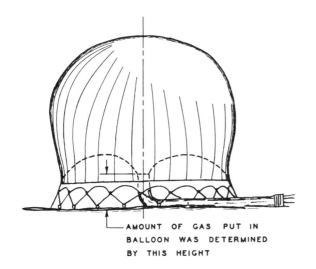

AMOUNT OF GAS PUT IN
BALLOON WAS DETERMINED
BY THIS HEIGHT

POSITION OF BALLOON
WHEN INFLATED WITH GAS

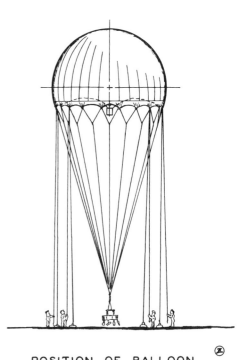

POSITION OF BALLOON
PRIOR TO LAUNCHING

Figure 81. Layout for anchoring and inflating bombing balloons for launching.

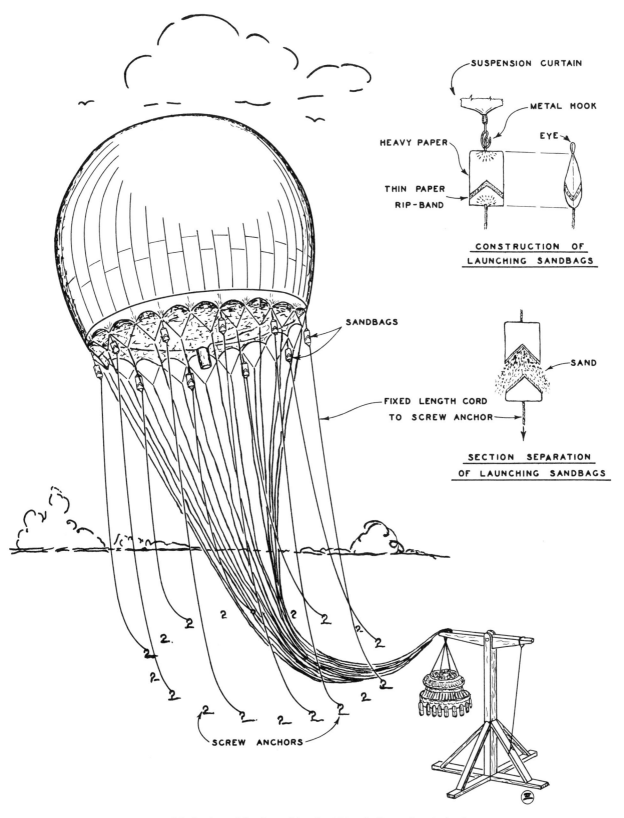

SUSPENSION CURTAIN

METAL HOOK

HEAVY PAPER

EYE

THIN PAPER
RIP-BAND

CONSTRUCTION OF
LAUNCHING SANDBAGS

SAND

SECTION SEPARATION
OF LAUNCHING SANDBAGS

SANDBAGS

FIXED LENGTH CORD
TO SCREW ANCHOR

SCREW ANCHORS

Figure 82.   Method used for launching bombing balloons in winds above two
and one-half miles per hour.

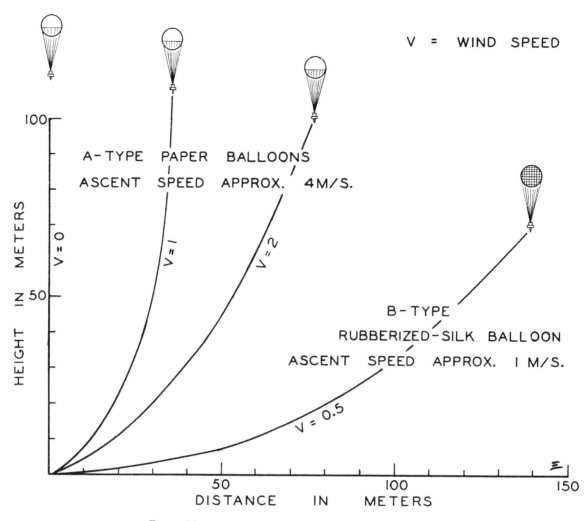

V = WIND SPEED

A-TYPE PAPER BALLOONS
ASCENT SPEED APPROX. 4M/S.

V = 0
V = 1
V = 2

B-TYPE
RUBBERIZED-SILK BALLOON
ASCENT SPEED APPROX. 1 M/S.

V = 0.5

Figure 83. Balloon ascent angle in relation to wind speed.

launching bags. Just before the foot ropes picked up the equipment load, the ropes between the launching sand-bags and crew anchors were taut. The shock load on the paper bags was sufficient to separate the sections of paper and release the sand. The balloon lifted the equipment load from the slot in the rocker arm of the wooden stand, and continued its ascent. The ascent was swift. Speed of about 200 m. (656 ft.) to 300 m. (984 ft.) per minute were attained, reaching the 10,000 m. (32,800 ft.) level in about 40 minutes.

Degree of Development

Balloon development continued until April 1945 with special emphasis placed on improving flight-control apparatus and method of production. The Japanese had not completed development of a satisfactory, low-cost, machine-made, raw, and laminated paper for the mass-produced balloon which would be comparable to the same materials made by hand. The balloon proper, of both types, presented no real problems, and development therefore would have been limited to refinements. Laboratory tests and data obtained from flight tests indicated that further development and refinement was required in the flight-control apparatus to reduce the percentage of flight failures.

War Casualties on United States Soil

Strict censorship in the newspapers and on radio concerning the paper bombing balloons prevented this vital intelligence information from reaching the Japanese. It also kept many Americans uniformed of the possible hazards associated with this unusual weapon. The area over which the bombs landed was so vast, considering their relatively small number, that the probability of personal contact was quite small. The law of averages did run out, however, on 5 May 1945 when a bomb from a balloon exploded and killed six people— four weeks after the Japanese had ended the balloon offensive.

The tragedy occurred in the Gearhart Mountain area just inside Lake County about sixty-five miles east-northeast of Klamath Falls, Oregon. The Reverend and Mrs. Archie Mitchell of Bly, Oregon, on that day took five children with them on an outing. While the Reverend Mr. Mitchell was moving the car, Mrs. Mitchell and the children found a strange object lying in the woods. They called to Mitchell, now a mere 40 feet away, and he shouted a warning, for he had heard rumors of Japanese balloons. Almost simultaneously one of the bombs detonated, killing Mrs. Mitchell and the children. The explosion produced a crater 12 inches deep, 15 inches wide, and 36 inches long. The incendiaries and demolition block were badly damaged by the blast, but did not explode.

Those killed were: *Mrs. Elsie Mitchell; Jay Gifford,* 12, son of Mr. and Mrs. J.N. Gifford; *Eddie Engen,* 13, son of Mr. and Mrs. Einar Engen; *Sherman Shoemaker,* 12, son of Mr. and Mrs. J.L. Shoemaker; and *Joan Patzke,* 11, and *Dick Patzke,* 13, daughter and son of Mr. and Mrs. Frank Patzke.

Forestry men who quickly gathered after the incident said the victims appeared to have been clustered around the balloon and someone must have tugged it enough to detonate a bomb.

Due to censorship, the only publicity permitted about the incident was that an unidentified object had exploded, killing six persons.

The six deaths were the only known fatalities on the United States mainland from enemy attack during World

Figure 84. Near Bly, Oregon, is the Mitchell Recreation Area, dedicated by the Weyerhaeuser Company to commemorate the six Americans that died there due to the explosion of a Japanese bomb balloon. The tragedy occurred 5 May 1945, nearly one month after the last balloon had been set adrift. Accidental triggering of the bomb-entangled balloon caused the mishap.

Figure 85. The Mitchell Recreation Area was established on 20 August 1950, one year after reparations were paid by our government to the next of kin of the casualties.

Figure 86. The bronze plaque inscription reads: "Dedicated/ to those/ who died here/ May 5, 1945/ by/ Japanese/ bomb explosion." Following the list of six names, it continues: "The only place/ on the/ American continent/ where death resulted/ from enemy action/ during World War II."

War II. In May 1949, the Senate Judiciary Committee approved a House-passed bill to pay $20,000 to the bereaved families. The bill, first introduced by Representative William Lemke, Republican, North Dakota, granted $5,000 to the widower of Mrs. Mitchell, and $3,000 to the parents of each of the children.

Senator Guy Gordon, Republican, Oregon, and other proponents of the measure said that the public had not been warned of the danger from the airborne bombs, although the armed services knew that several had reached this country.

The Weyerhaeuser Company, of Klamath Falls, Oregon, established the historic spot as a patriotic shrine, to be known as the Mitchell Recreation area. The dedication centered around a native-stone monument bearing a bronze plaque with the names of the victims. Other developments included outdoor fireplaces, appropriate signs for the memorial, and a protective iron fence around the site of the tragedy and monument. Thus, the United States paid another lasting tribute to its war dead.

Other American Observations

That only a small percentage of bombs reached North America can be attributed to malfunctioning of the ballast-control mechanism. A considerable number of the bomb-dropping devices recovered in the United States and Canada reportedly had a high percentage of the blowout plugs still in place in the periphery of the lower ring. This, apparently, was accountable to the failure of either the battery or fuse. Recoveries clearly indicated that the balloons could survive serious malfunctions of the ballast-dropping device and still arrive over the target. Such balloons, however, usually showed indications that some of the ballast sandbags and cargo had been pulled off by contact with the ground or water. Balloons on which the sequence of ballast dropping had stopped before the payload was released were not found to be a menace. Since the arming of the bomb would not take place until it was released from the carrying device, these bombs were usually inactive unless they were handled incautiously.

Much was learned from translations of inspection tags found on some of the balloons. Typical was the one found 13 March 1945 at Chimacum, Washington. The balloon was manufactured at the Sagami Army Arsenal, Factory No. 2 (about 15 miles northwest of Yokohama); the balloon number was 262; it had the classification "No. 102 Balloon"; the inscription was "passed with first-class rating"; the date of manufacture was February 1945, and it had been accepted 1 March 1945.

The 13-day period between acceptance and recovery date of the Chimacum balloon was almost the same as the period between the acceptance date of the Kalispell, Montana, balloon 31 October and its estimated landing date of 15 November 1944. They bore different tags.

A paper tag with Japanese characters was also found with the balloon, recovered at Hay River, Northwest Territory, Canada, on 12 June 1945 (the landing date is unknown). A translation of this tag revealed that "No. 11 balloon was manufactured on 23 January 1945 at Takaki factory." There are two cities named Takaki in Japan; one is in Miyagi Prefecture, approximately 25 miles northwest of Sendai, undoubtedly the factory location.

Another paper tag was found with the balloon fragment recovered near Mahogany, Oregon, on 9 June 1945 (date of landing unknown). A translation reads: No. 168 Balloon/ 31 January 1945/ 7 hours 50 minutes/ No. 10 Squadron.

A Japanese postcard was found in a sandbag ballast recovered near Bethel, Alaska, on 15 April 1945. The card was translated and appeared to be from a schoolboy to his father. It was addressed: Mr. Kazuo Shinada/ Hidano Butai, Toni Tai,/ c/o Ichinomiya Post Office,/ Chosei County, Chiba Prefecture. The card was from: Yoshiharu Shinada/ 4th Grade, Yawata Tai, Sakaiya Inn,/ Akayu Town, Kigashi County,/ Yamagata Prefecture.

Ichinomiya is about 40 miles southeast of Tokyo, and Akayu about 10 miles south of Sendai. Both locations were near possible sources of the ballast sand. Since there was no postmark visible on the card, it was impossible to say whether the card was mailed. The Hidano "Detachment" as used in the father's address, possibly carried the same name as Captain Monomichi Hidano, who commanded a material depot of a balloon regiment in March 1940. No further information is known about Captain Hidano.

Chronology of Balloon-bomb Incidents

(Information taken from G-2 Periodic Report No. 188, 4 August 1945)

Place	Recovery date	Remarks
1944		
1. Lat. 33:20 N, Long. 119.20 W	4 Nov.	Rubber balloon recorded at sea 66 miles southwest of San Pedro, California, at 1555 PWT by United States naval vessel. Envelope, rigging, and some apparatus recovered.
2. Kailua, Hawaii	14 Nov.	Paper balloon including envelope, rigging, and some apparatus recovered at sea 5 miles west of Kailua at 1000 HWT by the United States Coast Guard.

Place	Recovery date	Remarks
3. Thermopolis, Wyoming	6 Dec.	Fragments of a 15-kg. Japanese anti-personnel, high-explosive recovered as a result of this incident which occurred at 1800 MWT 6 December. An explosion occurred at this time followed by the sighting of what appeared to be a parachute descending to earth. A bright red flame was also seen by observers of the explosion. Bomb fragments were recovered from the scene of the incident about 15 miles northwest of Thermopolis on 7 December.
4. Kalispell, Montana	11 Dec.	Paper balloon including envelope, rigging, and some apparatus were recovered. This balloon was estimated to have landed between 11 and 25 November.
5. Manderson, Wyoming	19 Dec.	Piece of Japanese balloon paper measuring 3 x 4 feet.
6. Marshall, Alaska	23 Dec.	Paper balloon including 2 sandbags recovered 15 miles north of Marshall.
7. Holy Cross, Alaska	24 Dec.	Paper balloon found with most usual equipment.
8. Estacada, Oregon	31 Dec.	Paper balloon, including envelope, rigging, and small portion of the apparatus, was recovered. Balloon was estimated to have landed between 27 and 31 December.

1945

Place	Recovery date	Remarks
9. Stony Rapids, Saskatchewan, Canada	1 Jan.	Several fragments of balloon envelope found.
10. Medford, Oregon	4 Jan.	Fragments of what was identified as an incendiary-type bomb exploded in a field one mile south of Medford at 1740 PWT. A whistling sound as if a bomb was falling was heard prior to the explosion.
11. Sebastopol, California	4 Jan.	Paper balloon, including envelope fragments, rigging, and apparatus, landed at 1815 PWT.
12 At sea: 52:5 N, 160:00 W	5 Jan.	Merchant-vessel crew shot down white balloon of 30-foot diameter. Nothing recovered.
13. Napa, California	5 Jan.	Fragments of balloon fabric found (30 miles SE of Sebastopol). May have been part of incident No. 11.
14. Medford. Oregon	7 Jan.	Thermite bomb recovered.
15. Alturas, California	10 Jan.	Paper balloon, including envelope, rigging, and apparatus was forced down by a United States Navy airplane at 1750 PWT about 30 miles west of Alturas. Later inflated at Moffett Field, California. Presumably, this is the balloon shipped to the Naval Air Station Lakehurst, New Jersey, which finally came to the National Air and Space Museum for its collection (NASM 2436).
16. Adin, California	10 Jan.	Complete balloon with associated parts was found.
17. Minton, Saskatchewan, Canada	12 Jan.	Balloon descended 6 miles north of United States-Canadian border, released a 15-kg. bomb and two flares of incendiaries. One flare or incendiary exploded; the other and the bomb did not. Balloon then rose and disappeared. The incident occurred at 1630 MWT.
18. Lame Deer, Montana	13 Jan.	Paper balloon, including envelope and rigging, landed at 1600 MWT.
19. Ventura, California	15 Jan.	Fragments of a 15-kg., Japanese, anti-personnel, high-explosive bomb were recovered as a result of this incident. The bomb was observed to explode at 1800 PWT on 15 January at Saticoy, 8 miles east of Ventura. This bomb may have been dropped from the balloon recovered at Moorpark, 13 miles east of Saticoy.
20. Moorpark, California	15 Jan.	Paper balloon found about 15 miles east of the Ventura bomb explosion. Balloon was similar to others.
21. Moorpark, California	17 Jan.	Paper balloon, including envelope and rigging, was estimated to have landed between 15 January and 1230 PWT 17 January, when it was recovered. It was believed that this balloon possibly dropped the bomb that fell at Saticoy, California, 13 miles west of Moorpark on 15 January.
22. Fort Simpson, Northwest Territories, Canada	19 Jan.	Paper balloon, including envelope, rigging, and some apparatus, recovered. This balloon landed on 18 January.

Place	Recovery date	Remarks
23. Holy Cross, Alaska	21 Jan.	Paper balloon, including envelope, rigging part of the apparatus, and one sandbag, recovered 8 miles southwest of Holy Cross. It is believed this balloon landed 24 December 1944.
24. Shemya, Aleutian Islands	25 Jan.	Paper balloon with apparatus attached was shot down into the ocean approximately 40 miles southwest of Shemya Island by a fighter plane. This balloon, encountered at 28,000 feet, was not recovered.
25. Kashunuk, Alaska	30 Jan.*	Balloon-envelope fragment found.
26. Nogales, Arizona	31 Jan.*	Small fragment of balloon envelope found.
27. Julian, California	31 Jan.	Paper balloon, including envelope, rigging, and apparatus, recovered. The balloon landed at 1600 PWT.
28. Red Bluff, California	1 Feb.	Paper balloon, including a portion of the envelope and rigging, was recovered about 20 miles west of Red Bluff. This balloon landed between 1830 PWT 31 January and 1300 PWT 1 February.
29. Hayfork, California	1 Feb.	Paper balloon, including rigging, apparatus, seven sandbags, and four unexploded 10-pound incendiary bombs, recovered near Hayfork. This balloon landed about 1825 PWT. The envelope of this balloon was destroyed.
30. Laurence, Iowa	2 Feb.	Paper balloon, including envelope, rigging, and apparatus, was recovered.
31. Schuyler, Nebraska	2 Feb.	Piece of balloon paper, 5 x 6 feet in size, found.
32. Provost, Alberta, Canada	7 Feb.	Paper balloon, including envelope, rigging, and apparatus, recovered.
33. Newcastle, Wyoming	8 Feb.	Paper balloon, including envelope and rigging, recovered 25 miles west of Newcastle. This balloon landed at 1800 MWT.
34. Camp Beale, California	8 Feb.	Paper balloon, including apparatus, recovered 5 miles northwest of Marysville. The envelope and most of the rigging of this balloon, which landed at 1600 PWT, were destroyed.
35. Moose Jaw, Saskatchewan, Canada	9 Feb.	Paper balloon, including only the envelope and rigging, recovered.
36. Lodge Grass, Montana	9 Feb.	Paper balloon, including only the top third of the envelope, recovered. This balloon landed on the night of 8-9 February.
37. Hardin, Montana	12 Feb.	Bomb explosion followed by a ground fire occurred.
38. Riverdale, Montana	12 Feb.	Three bombs landed and exploded. Fragments indicated the bombs were incendiary.
39. Burwell, Nebraska	12 Feb.	Badly torn balloon envelope found with two incendiary bombs.
40. Nowlin, South Dakota	12 Feb.	Unexplained incendiary-bomb explosion occurred.
41. Cascade, Montana	12 Feb.	Bomb fragments smelling strongly of ammonia found.
42. Spokane, Washington	12 Feb.	Two unexploded bombs found 7 miles north of Spokane. These were believed to have been dropped only a short distance, as their paint was unmarred.
43. Calistoga, California	23 Feb.	Balloon shot down by aircraft. Paper fragment found at Elmira, California, about 35 miles away. [Out of sequence.]
44. Eden, Montana	13 Feb.	Paper balloon found, similar to others.
45. American Falls, Idaho	13 Feb.	Envelope only of a Japanese balloon found.
46. Hardin, Montana	13 Feb.	Balloon valve and shroud lines recovered.
47. Marie River, District of McKenzie, Canada	13 Feb.	Paper fragment found.
48. Prosser, Washington	15 Feb.	Paper balloon found with some of the usual apparatus.
49. Flathead Lake, Montana	17 Feb.	Long strip of paper found, believed to be part of a balloon envelope.
50. Deer Lodge, Montana	18 Feb.*	Two fragments of balloon envelope found.
51. Takla Lake, British Columbia, Canada	19 Feb.	Partially inflated balloon found.
52. Asotin, Washington	20 Feb.	Two-thirds of a balloon envelope and portions of shroud lines recovered.
53. Ephrata, Washington	21 Feb.	Balloon hit the ground, dropping pieces of altitude-control equipment. Balloon then rose and disappeared.
54. Spokane, Washington	21 Feb.	Two bombs (1 anti-personnel and 1 incendiary).
55. Sumas, Washington	21 Feb.	Balloon shot down by Royal Canadian Air Force aircraft. Recovered by Canadians.

*Indicates the estimated landing date.

Place	Recovery date	Remarks
56. Ashley, North Dakota	22 Feb.	Envelope and shroud lines found.
57. Ekwok, Alaska	22 Feb.	A balloon hit the ground, dropping a battery. Paper fragments found near Ekwok on 13 March.
58. Ephrata, Washington	22 Feb.	Parts of balloon were recovered.
59. Manyberries, Alberta, Canada	22 Feb.	Balloon found.
60. Hays, Montana	22 Feb.	Balloon with control apparatus found.
61. North Bend, Oregon	22 Feb.	Balloon shot down at 12,000 feet. Parts found later.
62. Kirby, Wyoming	22 Feb.	Balloon in good condition found.
63. Porcupine Plains, Saskatchewan, Canada	22 Feb.	Balloon with ballast-dropping equipment found.
64. Powell, Wyoming	22 Feb.	Damaged balloon found.
65. Glendo, Wyoming	22 Feb.	Damaged balloon with ballast-dropping apparatus found.
66. Chase, British Columbia, Canada	22 Feb.	Ballast-dropping apparatus and paper fragments recovered.
67. Ellsworth, Nebraska	22 Feb.	Valve and several pieces of shroud lines recovered.
68. Tremonton, Utah	23 Feb.	Balloon with damaged ballast-dropping apparatus found.
69. Rigby, Idaho	23 Feb.	Damaged balloon and ballast-dropping apparatus found.
70. Bigelow, Kansas	23 Feb.	Damaged balloon and ballast-dropping apparatus found.
71. Grand Rapids, Michigan	23 Feb.	Balloon envelope and shroud lines found.
72. Burns, Oregon	23 Feb.	Balloon with usual apparatus found.
73. Deer Island, Oregon	23 Feb.	Pieces of balloon envelope found following explosion.
74. Boyd, Montana	23 Feb.	Balloon envelope and ballast-dropping apparatus recovered.
75. Boise, Idaho	25 Feb.	Balloon envelope and ballast-dropping apparatus recovered.
76. Eugene, Oregon	26 Feb.	Damaged balloon envelope and control apparatus found.
77. Goldendale, Washington	27 Feb.	Pieces of balloon envelope and shroud lines found.
78. Bethel, Alaska	27 Feb.	Burned balloon envelope found 70 miles from Bethel.
79. Deer Island, Oregon (near St. Helens)	27 Feb.	Pieces of balloon found.
80. Lakebay, Washington	28 Feb.	Damaged envelope and ballast-dropping apparatus found.
81. Vaughn, Washington (Gig Harbor)	28 Feb.	Pieces of balloon and parts.
82. Holstein, Iowa	28 Feb.	Fragments of a 5-kg., candle-type, incendiary recovered.
83. Nanaimo, Vancouver Island, British Columbia, Canada	3 Mar.	Envelope, ballast-dropping apparatus, and bombs found.
84. Puyalup, Washington	3 Mar.	Paper fragments found.
85. Big Creek, British Columbia, Canada	4 Mar.*	Envelope, shroud lines, ballast-dropping device, and one unexploded 12-kg. (fin-type) incendiary.
86. Stuart Lake, British Columbia, Canada	5 Mar.	Paper fragments found.
87. Buffalo, South Dakota	6 Mar.	Shroud lines and several fragments of balloon envelope.
88. Bernice, Montana	10 Mar.	Balloon envelope and undercarriage.
89. Nelson House, Manitoba, Canada	10 Mar.	Bomb fragments found.
90. Wolf Creek, Oregon	10 Mar.	Bomb fragment found.
91. Galiano Island, British Columbia, Canada	10 Mar.	Balloon shot down; a second escaped.
92. Ephrata, Washington	10 Mar.	Balloon and ballast-dropping apparatus.
93. Satus Pass, Washington	10 Mar.	Balloon and ballast-dropping equipment.
94. Toppenish, Washington	10 Mar.	Burned envelope, shroud lines, and ballast-dropping equipment.
95. Nicola, British Columbia, Canada	10 Mar.	Balloon landed.
96. Vale, Oregon	10 Mar.	Envelope and shroud lines; believed to have landed at the time of an explosion sometime in January.
97. Cold Creek, Washington	10 Mar.	Balloon, complete, and parts.
98. Hammond, Montana	11 Mar.	Envelope and shroud lines.
99. Meridian, California	11 Mar.	Paper fragments found following balloon sighting and explosion.
100. Cold Creek, Washington	11 Mar.	Balloon and usual equipment.
101. Edson, Alberta, Canada	11 Mar.	Balloon landed.

*Indicates the estimated landing date.

Place	Recovery date	Remarks
102. Kunghit Island, Canada	11 Mar.	Balloon shot down.
103. West Cloverdale, California	12 Mar.	Paper fragments found.
104. Coal Harbor, Vancouver Island, British Columbia, Canada	12 Mar.	Balloon found.
105. At sea: 30°18'N, 132°52'W	12 Mar.	Balloon recovered by surface vessel.
106. Oxford House, Manitoba, Canada	12 Mar.	Balloon envelope, shroud lines, and ballast-dropping apparatus.
107. Whitehall, Montana	12 Mar.	Envelope and ballast-dropping equipment.
108. Baril Lake, Alberta, Canada	13 Mar.	Balloon recovered.
109. Port Hardy, Vancouver Island, British Columbia, Canada	13 Mar.	Balloon shot down; a second escaped.
110. Gambell, St. Lawrence Island, Alaska	13 Mar.	Paper fragment.
111. Legg, Montana	13 Mar.	Badly damaged balloon and other usual equipment.
112. Divide, Montana	13 Mar.	Balloon and ballast-dropping equipment.
113. Farmington, Washington	13 Mar.	Balloon.
114. Echo, Oregon	13 Mar.	Balloon; now in the National Air and Space Museum (NASM 617).
115. Paine Field, Everett, Washington	13 Mar.	A badly damaged balloon and ballast-dropping apparatus.
116. Bechland, Montana	13 Mar.	Balloon envelope and shroud lines.
117. American Falls, Idaho	13 Mar.	Shroud lines and fragments of a balloon were found following the report that a balloon was seen exploding in the air.
118. Malheur Lake, Oregon	13 Mar.	Damaged balloon and ballast-dropping equipment.
119. Chimacum, Washington	13 Mar.	Balloon, ballast-dropping equipment, and a bomb.
120. Phillips, Alaska	13 Mar.	Damaged envelope and shroud lines.
121. Delta, Colorado	13 Mar.	Envelope fragments and shroud lines found following an explosion.
122. Harlowton, Montana	13 Mar.	Bomb found; preliminary reports indicated it was of the candle-type incendiary.
123. Ontario, Oregon	13 Mar.	Pieces of balloon and parts.
124. Gambier Island, British Columbia	14 Mar.	Paper fragments found.
125. Yamhill, Oregon	14 Mar.	Paper fragments found following explosion.
126. Pocahontas, Iowa	14 Mar.	Damaged envelope and shroud lines.
127. Grimes, California	14 Mar.	Balloon, with complete equipment recovered. Also recovered were one fin-type and one candle-type incendiary.
128. Hay Lake, Alberta, Canada	14 Mar.	Pieces of bakelite and empty sandbag.
129. Big Bend, California	14 Mar.	Part of envelope, shroud lines, and valve.
130. Mumtrak, Alaska	15 Mar.	Balloon envelope and valve assembly.
131. Williams Lake, British Columbia, Canada	15 Mar.*	Balloon envelope.
132. Chase, British Columbia, Canada	15 Mar.	Damaged envelope, valve, and ballast-dropping device.
133. Baker Creek, British Columbia, Canada	15 Mar.	Two small fragments of balloon envelope.
134. Coquille, Oregon	15 Mar.	Pieces of balloon found.
135. Coram, Montana	16 Mar.	Paper fragments found.
136. Fort Babine, British Columbia, Canada	17 Mar.	Shroud lines and envelope.
137. Sula, Montana	17 Mar.	Bomb fragments found.
138. Kinak, Alaska	18 Mar.	Two explosions heard; paper fragments found.
139. Alexis Creek, British Columbia, Canada	18 Mar *	Large fragment of balloon envelope reported found.
140. Guerneville, California	18 Mar.	Paper fragment found.
141. Glen, Montana	18 Mar.	Bomb fragments found.
142. The Dalles, Oregon	18 Mar.	Bomb fragments found.
143. Garrison, Utah	18 Mar.	Balloon and ballast-dropping equipment found.
144. Laurel, Montana	18 Mar.	Balloon envelope and most of the other usual equipment.
145. Marie Lake, Manitoba, Canada	19 Mar.	Balloon found.
146. Cedarvale, British Columbia, Canada	19 Mar.	Balloon found.
147. Sonoyta, Sonora, Mexico	19 Mar.	Balloon found.
148. Timnath, Colorado	20 Mar.	Fragments of two bombs found.
149. Chadron, Nebraska	20 Mar.	Envelope and ballast-dropping equipment.

*Indicates the estimated landing date.

Place	Recovery date	Remarks
150. Fort Chipewyan, Alberta, Canada	20 Mar.	Balloon found.
151. William Lake, Manitoba, Canada	20 Mar.	Envelope and ballast-dropping equipment.
152. Denman Island, British Columbia, Canada	20 Mar.	Balloon and candle-type incendiary bomb.
153. Olds, Alberta, Canada	20 Mar.*	Fragments of a 5-kg (candle-type) incendiary.
154. Wimborne, Alberta, Canada	20 Mar.	Bomb fragments found.
155. Foremost, Alberta, Canada	20 Mar.	Balloon envelope and parts of ballast-dropping apparatus.
156. The Dalles, Oregon	20 Mar.	Incendiary bomb found.
157. Delburne, Alberta, Canada	20 Mar.	Bomb fragments found.
158. Gillette, Wyoming	21 Mar.	Part of balloon enveloped recovered.
159. Murphy, Oregon	21 Mar.	Balloon found.
160. Dillingham, Alaska	21 Mar.	Balloon found.
161. Camsell Portage, Saskatchewan, Canada	21 Mar.	Balloon found.
162. Glen, Montana	21 Mar.	Bomb seen falling and explosion heard.
163. Reno, Nevada	22 Mar.	Balloon shot down. Explosion on landing. Two incendiary bombs of candle type were recovered intact nearby.
164. Rogerson, Idaho	22 Mar.	Envelope and ballast-dropping equipment found.
165. Ashcroft, British Columbia, Canada	22 Mar.	Balloon found.
166. Volcano, California	22 Mar.	Envelope and ballast-dropping equipment.
167. Basin, Wyoming	22 Mar.	Paper fragment found.
168. Rome, Oregon	22 Mar.	Envelope, ballast-dropping apparatus, battery, valve, and other parts.
169. Ree Heights, South Dakota	22 Mar.	Balloon found.
170. Barrier Lake, British Columbia, Canada	23 Mar.	Balloon found.
171. Desdemona, Texas	23 Mar.	Balloon found.
172. Bethel, Alaska	23 Mar.	Envelope valve found.
173. Athabasca, Alberta, Canada	23 Mar.	Balloon reported found.
174. Delburne, Alberta, Canada	23 Mar.	Portion of balloon envelope and shroud lines.
175. Desdemona, Texas	23 Mar.	Bomb fragments found.
176. Britain River, British Columbia, Canada	24 Mar.	Portion of balloon envelope.
177. Osceola, Nebraska	24 Mar.	Balloon found.
178. Woodson, Texas	24 Mar.	Portion of balloon envelope and shroud lines.
179. Hanson Island, British Columbia, Canada	25 Mar.*	Fragment of balloon envelope reported recovered.
180. Farmington, Michigan	25 Mar.*	Fragments of a 5-kg, candle-type incendiary bomb found.
181. Kadoka, South Dakota	26 Mar.	Numerous small pieces of balloon envelope found.
182. Strathmore, Alberta, Canada	28 Mar.	Pieces of balloon envelope, valve, and shroud lines.
183. Laguna Salada, Baja California, Mexico	28 Mar.	Balloon shot down.
184. Whitewater, British Columbia, Canada	28 Mar.	Balloon reported recovered.
185. Canol Rd., Yukon Territory, Canada	29 Mar.	Fragments of an exploded, 15-kg, high-explosive bomb.
186. Adrian, Oregon	29 Mar.	Anti-personnel bomb found.
187. Nyssa, Oregon	29 Mar.	Bomb recovered.
188. Pyramid Lake, Nevada	29 Mar.	Envelope, shroud lines, ballast-dropping apparatus, valve, and other parts recovered.
189. Duchesne, Utah	30 Mar.	Balloon envelope and shroud lines recovered.
190. Grafton, North Dakota	30 Mar.	Envelope, shroud lines, valve, and other parts.
191. Bozeman, Montana	30 Mar.	Envelope, valve, ballast-dropping apparatus, and sandbags.
192. Consul, Saskatchewan, Canada	30 Mar.	Ballast-dropping apparatus and bomb fragments.
193. Waterhen Lake, Manitoba, Canada	30 Mar.	Balloon envelope and valve.
194. Red Elm, South Dakota	30 Mar.	Balloon envelope and ballast-dropping apparatus.
195. Marcus, South Dakota	31 Mar.	Bomb fragment found.

*Indicates the estimated landing date

Place	Recovery date	Remarks
196. Ituna, Saskatchewan, Canada	31 Mar.	Envelope, shroud lines, and demolition charge.
197. Dillon, Montana	1 Apr.*	Parts of balloon envelope, shroud lines, and valve.
198. Tampico, Washington	1 Apr.*	Fragments of balloon envelope, ballast-dropping device, and one 5-kg, candle-type incendiary.
199. Hoopa Indian Reservation, California	1 Apr.*	Badly damaged envelope, shroud lines, valve, ballast-dropping device, battery, aneroids, and demolition block.
200. Hay River, District of McKenzie, Canada	1 Apr.*	Fragment of balloon envelope, ballast-dropping device, 7 sandbags, and two, unexploded, 5-kg, candle-type incendiaries.
201. Colville, Washington	1 Apr.	Balloon envelope recovered.
202. Harper, Oregon	3 Apr.	Portions of balloon envelope, shroud lines, valve, and suspension skirt band.
203. Walla Walla, Washington	3 Apr.	Balloon envelope and ballast-dropping apparatus, valve, and other parts.
204. Massacre Lake, Nevada	5 Apr.	Envelope, shroud lines, ballast-dropping apparatus, valve, and other parts.
205. Turner, Montana	6 Apr.	Balloon with undercarriage recovered.
206. Provolt, Oregon	7 Apr.	Pieces of balloon found.
207. Merritt, British Columbia, Canada	8 Apr.	Balloon envelope, shroud lines, and valve recovered.
208. Southern Indian Lake, Manitoba, Canada	10 Apr.	Balloon envelope and other parts.
209. Plane, Idaho	10 Apr.	Sand ballast bag and iron hook reported found.
210. Bald Mountain, Oregon	10 Apr.*	Envelope, ballast-dropping device, two sandbags, one 12-kg (fin-type) and four 5-kg, candle-type incendiaries all unexploded.
211. Attu, Aleutian Islands, Alaska	12 Apr.	Balloon shot down.
212. Rome, Oregon	12 Apr.	Complete balloon and parts.
213. Attu, Aleutian Islands, Alaska	13 Apr.	Nine balloons shot down; one recovered.
214. Little Sitkin, Aleutian Islands, Alaska	13 Apr.	Balloon shot down.
215. Wolsey, South Dakota	13 Apr.	Large paper fragment.
216. Midas Creek, Alaska	15 Apr.	Shroud lines and ballast-dropping apparatus reported.
217. At sea: 52°46'N, 178°30'W	15 Apr.	Balloon shot down.
218. Bethel, Alaska	15 Apr.	Two boxes (possibly aneroid containers) found.
219. Amchitka, Aleutian Islands, Alaska	15 Apr.	Envelope, ballast-dropping apparatus, valve, shroud lines, and other parts.
220. Tyee, Oregon	15 Apr.	Pieces of balloon.
221. Snowville, Utah	16 Apr.	Large paper fragment found.
222. Platinum, Alaska	16 Apr.	Balloon reported shot down.
223. Boundary Bay, British Columbia, Canada	17 Apr.	Balloon reported grounded.
224. Morica Lake, British Columbia, Canada	17 Apr.	Balloon envelope, ballast-dropping device, 22 sandbags, shroud lines, valve, and two, unexploded, 5-kg, candle-type incendiaries.
225. Wapato, Washington	19 Apr.	Pieces of balloon recovered.
226. Tikchik Lake, Alaska	20 Apr.	Balloon envelope, damaged valve, ballast-dropping device, aneroid box, demolition block, and other parts.
227. Vedder Mt., British Columbia, Canada	20 Apr.	Balloon reported grounded.
228. Watson Lake, Yukon Territory, Canada	20 Apr.	Parts of balloon reported found.
229. Chilliwack, British Columbia, Canada	20 Apr.	Envelope and shroud lines.
230. Elko, Nevada	21 Apr.	Balloon reported recovered.
231. Phillipsburg, Montana	21 Apr.	Balloon reported found.
232. At sea: 53°3'N, 135°52'W	23 Apr.	Balloon of rubberized fabric found.
233. Lake of the Woods, Oregon	23 Apr.	Envelope, shroud lines, ballast-dropping apparatus, battery, and other parts recovered.

*Indicates the estimated landing date.

Place	Recovery date	Remarks
234. Kitchener, British Columbia, Canada	24 Apr.	Envelope and shroud lines recovered.
235. Paragonah, Utah	25 Apr.	Paper fragment found.
236. Beatty, Oregon	26 Apr.	Paper fragment found.
237. Akiak, Alaska	28 Apr.	Balloon reported recovered.
238. Moxee City, Washington	30 Apr.	Balloon parts recovered.
239. Huntington, Oregon	2 May	Pieces of balloon recovered.
240. Bly, Oregon	5 May	Balloon, complete with parts, (Incident involving bomb explosion, killing five children and one woman.)
241. Stettler, Alberta, Canada	5 May	Fragments of balloon envelope found.
242. Enterprise, Oregon	12 May	Incendiary bomb recovered.
243. Kelvington, Saskatchewan, Canada	15 May	Gas-release valve and ballast-dropping device.
244. Chilliwack, British Columbia, Canada	20 May	Balloon envelope, shroud lines, valve, ballast-dropping device, 2 sandbags, one unexploded, 12-kg, tin-type, and two unexploded, 5-kg, candle-type incendiaries.
245. Enterprise, Oregon	21 May	Pieces of balloon.
246. Milo, Alberta, Canada	23 May	Several fragments of balloon envelope.
247. Asotin, Washington	25 May	Pieces of balloon and parts.
248. Harper, Oregon	25 May	Pieces of balloon and parts.
249. Madison, South Dakota	26 May	Unexploded, 5-kg, candle-type incendiary bomb.
250. Summer Lake, Oregon	26 May	Small fragments of balloon envelope, shroud lines, and suspension skirt band.
251. Vanderhoof, British Columbia, Canada	26 May	Several balloon-envelope fragments found.
252. Soldier Mt., California	26 May	Fragments of balloon envelope found.
253. High River, Alberta, Canada	28 May	Damaged envelope and ballast-dropping device.
254. Chilanko River, British Columbia, Canada	29 May	Portions of balloon envelope, two, 5-kg, candle-type incendiaries, and other parts.
255. Pryor, Montana	1 Jun.	Fragment of balloon envelope found.
256. Jordan Valley, Oregon	7 Jun.	Several small fragments of balloon envelope.
257. Mahogany, Oregon	8 Jun.	Pieces of balloon and parts found.
258. Mahogany, Oregon	9 Jun.	Fragment of balloon envelope reported found.
259. Collbran, Colorado	12 Jun.	Small fragment of balloon envelope found.
260. Egegik, Alaska	14 Jun.	Balloon reported grounded.
261. Skukuma Creek, British Columbia, Canada	15 Jun.	Fragment of balloon envelope found.
262. Whitecourt, Alberta, Canada	15 Jun.	Two fragments of balloon envelope found.
263. Mayo, Yukon Territory, Canada	16 Jun.	Several fragments of envelope found.
264. Anchorage, Alaska	18 Jun.	Balloon envelope, valve, ballast-dropping device, three sandbags, one unexploded high-explosive bomb, and two unexploded, 5-kg, candle-type incendiaries.
265. Mahood Lake, British Columbia, Canada	18 Jun.	Fragments of balloon envelope found.
266. Tampico, Montana	21 Jun.	Balloon, complete with parts.
267. Yank, British Columbia, Canada	23 Jun.	Fragments of a balloon envelope found.
268. Gilmore, Idaho	24 Jun.	Balloon envelope and shroud lines recovered.
269. Hailey, Idaho	24 Jun.	Balloon envelope, shroud lines, and ballast-dropping device.
270. Old Crow River, Yukon Territory, Canada	24 Jun.	Portions of balloon envelope reported found.
271. Dease Lake, British Columbia, Canada	27 Jun.	Balloon and three 5-kg, candle-type incendiaries, two exploded and one unexploded.
272. Ajo, Arizona	2 Jul.	Damaged envelope, shroud lines, and valve.
273. Boulder, Montana	4 Jul.	About one-fourth of balloon envelope found.
274. Lake Hyatt, Oregon	5 Jul.	Balloon and parts found.

Place	Recovery date	Remarks
275. Alberni, Vancouver Island, British Columbia, Canada	5 Jul.	Balloon envelope, valve, ballast-dropping device, one unexploded 15-kg, high-explosive bomb, and one unexploded incendiary.
276. Lake Hyatt, Oregon	5 Jul.	Damage envelope, valve ballast-dropping device, one unexploded 5-kg (candle-type) incendiary, and other parts.
277. Monida, Montana	6 Jul.	Balloon envelope and shroud lines.
278. Aishihik, Yukon Territory, Canada	11 Jul.	Balloon envelope, valve, ballast-dropping device, and shroud lines.
279. Jiggs, Nevada	12 Jul.	Balloon envelope, shroud lines, aneroids, and ballast-dropping device.
280. Salmo, British Columbia, Canada	16 Jul.	Shroud lines and fragments of balloon envelope reported found.
281. Mount Pitt, Oregon	18 Jul.	Incendiary bomb. (Possibly related to Lake of the Woods incident of 23 April 1945.)
282. Lillooet, British Columbia, Canada	19 Jul.	Balloon envelope and shroud lines reported found.
283. At sea (430 mi. ESE of Tokyo)	19 Jul.	A balloon was shot down by a navy aircraft; it sank before recovery.
284. Mount Pitt, Oregon	20 Jul.	Unexploded 5-kg (candle-type) incendiary found.
285. Indian Springs, Nevada	20 Jul.	Balloon envelope, shroud lines, and valve.

Summary of Positive Incidents Reported*
(4 November 1944 to 28 July 1945)

Location	Nov.-Dec. Jan.	Feb.	Mar.	Apr.	May	June	July
ALASKA (including Aleutian Islands)	5	2	6	9(+8)		2	
CANADA							
Alberta		2	11		3	1	
British Columbia		2	20	6	3	4	3
District of McKenzie	1	1	1	1			
Manitoba			5	1			
Saskatchewan	2	2	3		1		
Yukon Territory			1	1		2	1
UNITED STATES							
Arizona	1						1
California	10	4	6	1	1		
Colorado			2			1	
Idaho		3	2	1		2	
Iowa		2	1				
Kansas		1					
Michigan		1	1				
Montana	2	10	13	3		2	2
Nebraska		3	2				
Nevada			2	2			2
North Dakota		1	1				
Oregon	3	4	13	7	6	3	4
South Dakota		1	5	1	1		
Texas			3				
Utah		1	2	2			
Washington		10	9	5	1		
Wyoming	2	4	2				
MEXICO			2				
HAWAII	1						
OTHERS (at sea)	1		1	2			1
Total	28	54	114	42	16	17	14

*When possible, the known or estimated landing date is used. Where neither is available, the recovery date is used.

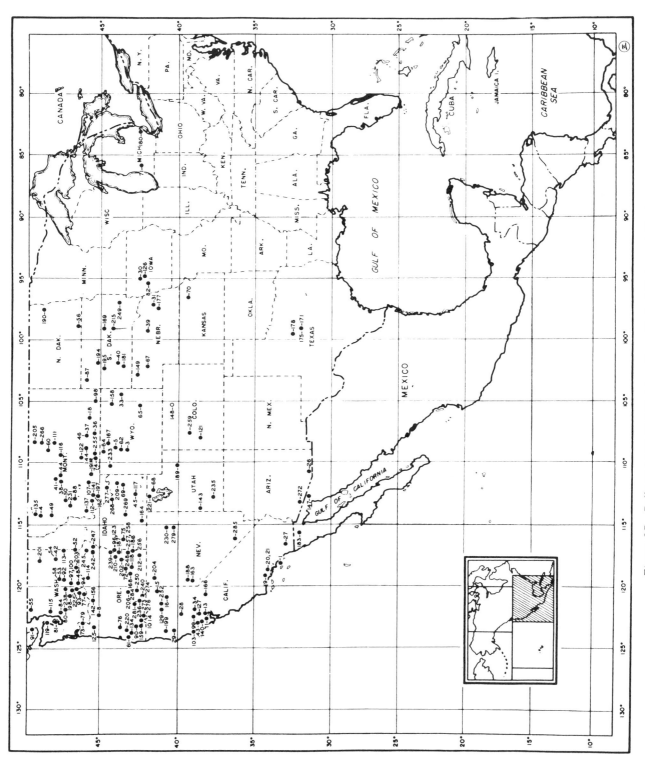

Figure 87. Balloon-bomb incident locations. United States and Mexico.

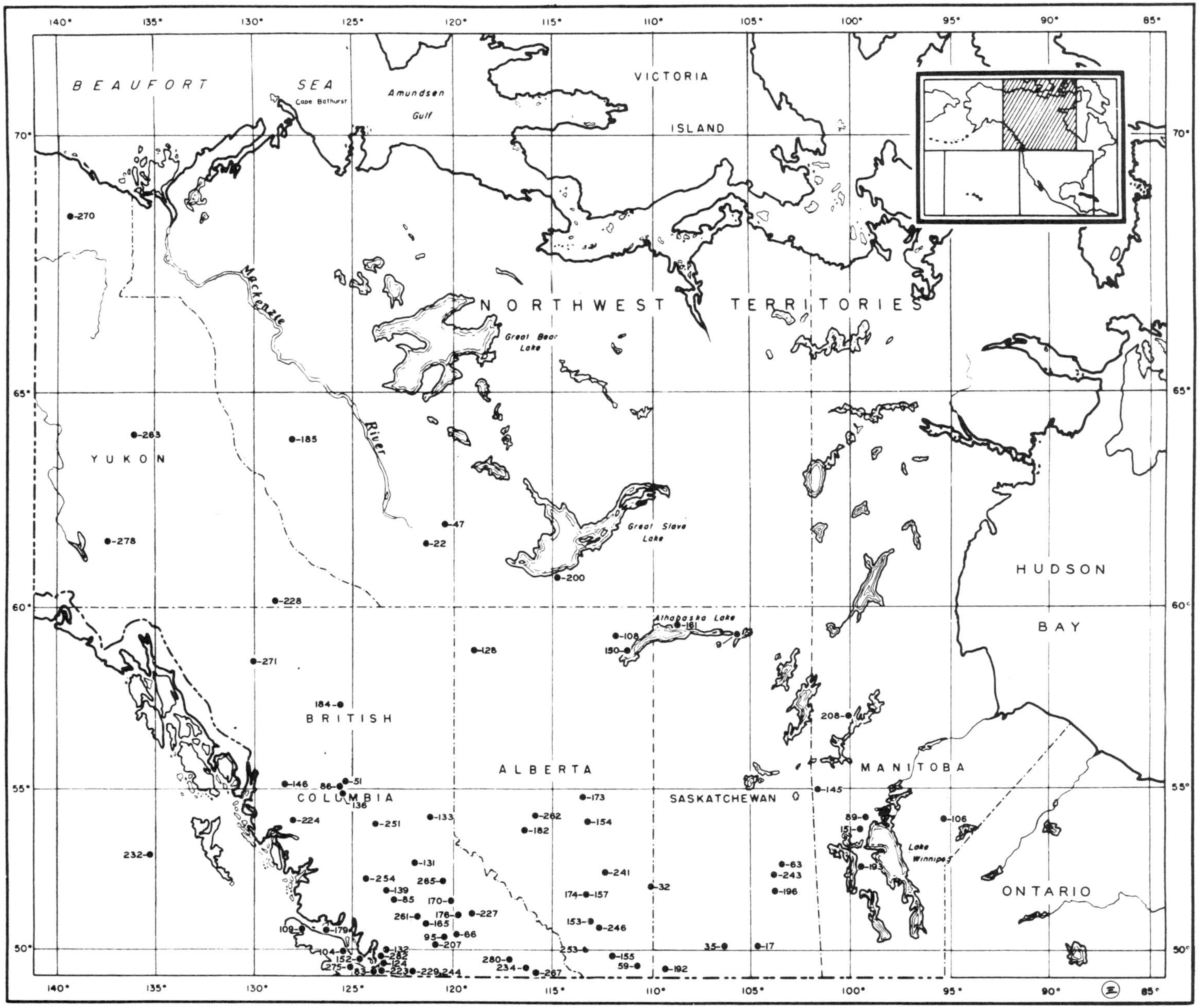

Figure 88. Balloon-bomb incident locations. Canada.

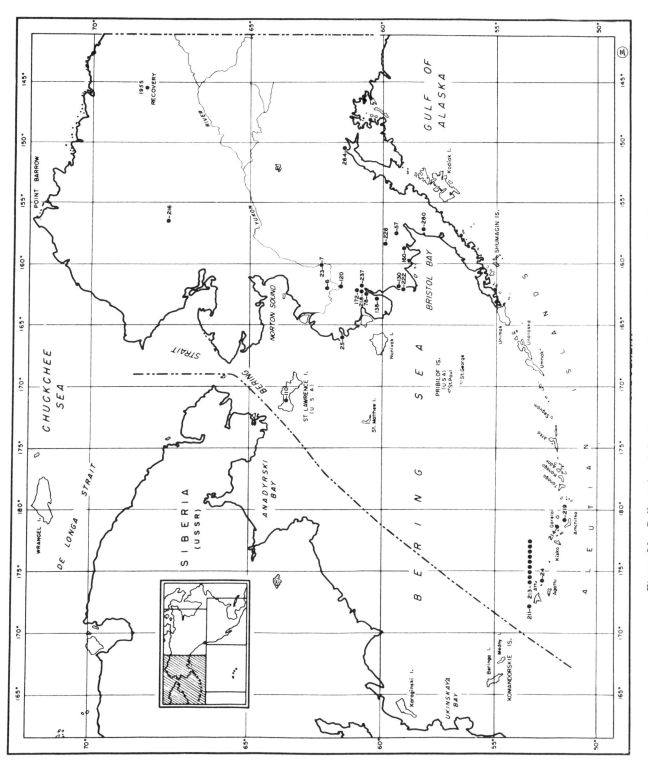

Figure 89. Balloon-bomb incident locations. Alaska and the Aleutian islands.

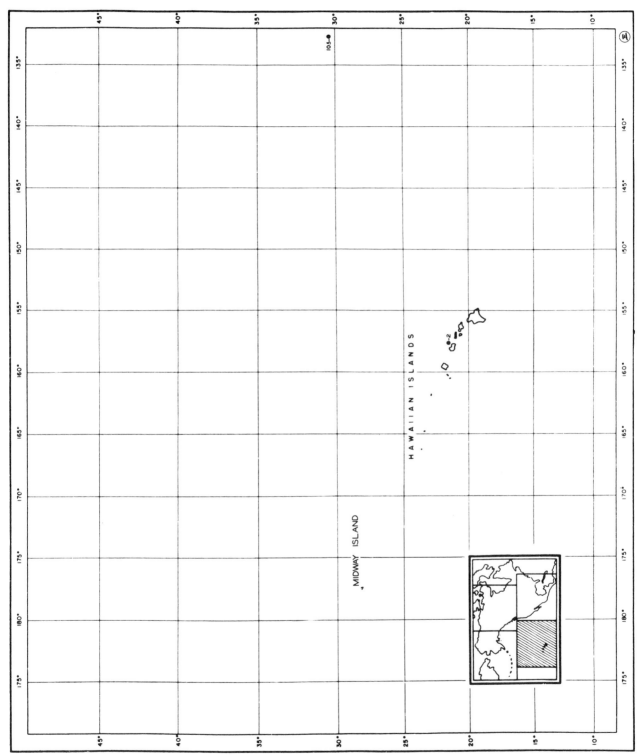

Figure 90. Balloon-bomb incident locations. Hawaii.

81

Epilogue

While the bold experiment with the balloon bomb is now history, the dangers of the balloon bomb still may exist. Hundreds of these bombs were never found and may still be detonated with the slightest contact.

On 1 January 1955, the Department of Defense released word that such a bomb, "still highly explosive and dangerous even after exposure ... for nearly a decade," had been found in Alaska. This news release is further quoted in part:

> Flying low between Barter Island and Fort Yukon, Don Hulshizer, Chief Bush Pilot for Wien Alaska Airlines, Fairbanks, Alaska, spotted a dull white object on the ground near the Scheenjek River. He decreased altitude in an attempt at identification, but because of the rough terrain he was unable to distinguish the object clearly.
>
> Surmising that the find was either a parachute or part of a downed aircraft, Hulshizer contacted Air Intelligence officers at Ladd Air Force Base near Fairbanks, Alaska. Attempts by L-20 and SA-16 search craft to relocate the strange object at first proved unavailing due to the thick carpet and tundra-brush and undergrowth. Finally sighted and pinpointed, Air Force officers determined that the best chance for its recovery lay in a helicopter operation. The 74th Air Rescue Squadron at Ladd supplied a H-5 helicopter as well as a SA-16 aircraft to fly protective cover on the 230-mile trip.
>
> The helicopter was unable to land, but Lt. Harold L. Hale, of Pueblo, Colorado, an intelligence technician with the 504th Air Intelligence Squadron, dropped to the ground. He too thought it was a parachute but after discovering the "chute" was made of paper and that the gondola was most unusual, he was reasonably sure it was of Japanese origin. He stuffed the balloon under a tree so it would not be reported again as an unidentified object, and loaded the remaining 120 pounds of the strange object into the hovering helicopter. The device was sent to Wright-Patterson AFB, for closer inspection, and it was discovered that the explosives were still quite potent even after the many years of exposure on the ground in the northwest woods.

A brief examination of maps showing downed-balloon locations reveals that the more populated and traveled areas show the largest number discovered. It would be safe to assume that the same intensity would prevail over the adjacent wilderness and therefore hundreds of balloons and their bombs have yet to be discovered. Experts say there is no way of knowing how long these uncovered bombs will continue to be highly explosive. Hunters, hikers, and fishermen are especially warned to report the location of any bombs found to the nearest military installation without delay.

It would be the supreme irony if any more American lives were lost to the "Fu-Go Weapon" revenge bomb of a war the world wants to forget.

Bibliography

Arakawa, H. *Basic Principles of the Balloon Bomb.* Meteorological Research Institute, Tokyo, Japan, January 1956. 5 pp.

"Balloon Bomb in Alaska." *New York Herald-Tribune,* 2 January 1945.

"Balloons . . . But Japan Never Knew Outcome." *New York Times,* 29 May 1947.

"Blast Kills 6." *Herald and News* (Klamath Falls, Oregon), 7 May 1945.

"Bomb-Laden Balloons Fizzle." *New York Times,* 16 August 1945.

Conley, Cornelius W. "The Great Japanese Balloon Offensive." *Air University Review,* February-March 1968, pp. 68-83.

Davis, Jack. "Japanese History Relived." *The Afterburner* (Yokota Air Base, Japan), 18 October 1963.

Groueff, Stephane. *Manhattan Project: The Untold Story of the Making of the Atomic Bomb.* Pp. 353-355. New York: Bantam Books, 1968.

Hirata, Tatsu, [Paper-made ICBMs.] *Koku Fan Magazine,* September 1964, pp. 67-73. [In Japanese.]

"Japanese Balloons." Chapter 10. *Fourth Air Force Historical Study No. III-2,* pp. 501-516. [n.d.]

"Japanese Balloons Sighted—First Complete Story." *Herald and News* (Klamath Falls, Oregon), 17 August 1945.

"Japanese Free Balloons." Army Service Forces, Hq. 4th Service Command, (10 July 1945), 14 pp. [Unpublished manuscript.]

"Japanese Free Balloons." *Western Defense Command Intelligence Study,* No. 1 (10 February 1945). 55 pp. [Unpublished manuscript.]

"Japanese Free Balloons and Related Incidents." Military Intelligence Division, War Department. Reports 1 through 8. [Unpublished manuscript.]

"Japanese Paper Balloon" Guggenheim Aeronautics Laboratory, Report for Western Sea Frontier (4 April 1945). 44 pp. [Unpublished manuscript, n.d.]

LaPaz, Lincoln. "Japan's Balloon Invasion of America." *Colliers,* 17 January 1953, pp. 9-11.

McKay, H.W. "Japanese Paper Balloons." *The Engineering Journal,* September 1945, pp. 563-567.

Mineralogy and Some of Its Applications. pp. 17-18. Cambridge, Mass.: Mineralogical Society of America, Harvard University [n.d.; pamphlet].

"9000 Balloon Bombs Against U.S." *Washington Post,* 16 January 1946.

"Piccard Flies Japanese Paper Balloon." *New York Times,* 17 February 1947.

"Raids by Japanese Balloons." *New York Times,* 9 February 1946.

"A Report on Japanese Free Balloons." *Coast Artillery Journal,* March-April 1946. 4 pp.

[A Report on the Research of the Bombing Balloon.] Ninth Military Laboratory, Weapon Administration Bureau, October 1945. [In Japanese.]

Takada, Teiji. [Balloon Bomb, I.] *Shizen,* vol. 6, no. 1 (January 1951), pp. 24-33. [In Japanese.]

_____. [Balloon Bomb, II.] *Shizen,* vol. 6, no. 2 (February 1951), pp. 44-54. [In Japanese.]

_____. [Balloon Bomb, III.] *Shizen,* vol. 6, no. 3 (March 1951), pp. 70-77. [In Japanese.]

Weidner, George E. "Japanese Bombing Balloons." *Technical and Technological Survey* (United States Army), PB Report 28880, (2 January 1946). 32 pp.

Wilbur, H.W. "Those Japanese Balloons." *Readers Digest,* vol. 57, no. 8 (August 1950), pp. 23-26.

Index